MW01047999

Sketches in the History of
By Eber Pettit

i

INTRODUCTORY.

Slavery in the United States after the Fugitive Slave law was enacted, assumed its most hideous aspect. When in colonial times it pervaded more or less all the colonies, it was not regarded as a special source of profit, and the value was but little more than nominal. After the adoption of the Constitution, State after State provided for its abolition till it was finally limited to the States south of Mason & Dixon's line and the Ohio river. The invention of the cotton gin and the profitableness of the culture of cane and cotton enhanced the value of slave property, and so far increased the demand for this kind of labor that the raising of slaves for the Southern market became a large source of income to the northern Slave States. In process of time they were held as mere chattels, without legal rights, and could not make bargains, marriage contracts, or perform any act whatever in which the law granted them any protection. In the eye of the law they were as much property as horses and cattle. This legal ownership enabled the masters to supply the slave auctions with human chattels, and caused great anguish to the poor wretches who were subject to sale and separation of kindred with no legal redress against any cruelty which might be inflicted. In the District of Columbia was a large slave mart, but it was so repugnant to Northern sentiments that finally the traffic was abolished there, but was continued at Alexandria, which was receded to Virginia.

At an early date the moral sense of many of the people of the North was aroused to the enormity of the crime of slavery and measures were taken for its abolition. The first slaves brought to this country were sold from a Dutch vessel at Jamestown, Va., in 1619. There were twenty of them. From that time up to 1776 three hundred thousand were imported. In the Continental Congress it was resolved that no more slaves should be brought to this country, but on the adoption of the

Constitution, Congress was prohibited from abolishing the slave trade till 1808. In the meantime Anti-Slavery Societies were formed in several States, and Benj. Franklin was President of such an organization. The Quakers persistently protested against human bondage, and petitioned the Convention to provide in the Constitution for its abolition. It was supposed at that time that human bondage would cease in a few years.

In this philanthropists were disappointed, as its rapid growth will show. In 1790 as seen by the census the slaves numbered 697,897, which was more than double the number at the commencement of the Revolutionary war.

In 1861 the war commenced between the Northern and Southern States, which resulted in the abrogation of all property title to more than four millions of human beings in the United States and territories As one after another the Northern States abolished slavery, they became an asylum for fugitives from the institution in the Southern States. On the 4th of July, 1827, all slaves held in the State of New York were set at liberty by an act passed in 1817. Thereafter all the States bordering on the lakes and rivers between the United States and Canada were free States. In all these States were found friends of the oppressed race, who desired their emancipation, and the fugitives from slavery found assistance and protection among these philanthropists, a large number of whom were Quakers who had always earnestly protested against human bondage. Still the refugees from slavery were not safe in the free States. The Constitution provided for their surrender, and the U. S. laws designated the manner of procedure. Rewards were offered for their return, and many people were found who for the pecuniary inducements were willing to participate in this business. The fugitives were not secure till they reached the soil of

Canada. An effort was made for a treaty with Great Britain to secure their return from Canada, but without success.

After the passage of the fugitive slave law, the danger of capture was enhanced and many left the free States for greater safety who had long been residents in them.

Notwithstanding the rewards and penalties of the law, fugitives still continued to escape, and endured untold suffering in pursuing their trackless course, often through an unbroken wilderness, guided by the north star to the land of freedom beyond the dominion of the stars and stripes. For some forty years these pilgrims to the land of liberty made their way through the Northern States and across the border. Scattered through the country were humanitarian people who believed in the "higher law," and that the complexion of the individual should not exclude him from the enjoyment of his "inalienable rights." These people protected the fleeing fugitive, secreted him from his pursuers, and conducted him from station to station till he was landed in Canada. The secrecy with which they managed the matter and the certainty of the delivery of the passengers on their line, gave by common consent the name of the *Underground Railroad*. The number of those who escaped is a wonder, in view of the difficulties encountered. It is estimated by a prominent refugee from Kentucky, who made his escape in 1836, that fully *thirty-five thousand* fugitives have reached Canada from the Slave States. As would be expected, only the shrewdest, able bodied and most enterprising would succeed. They secured land in the home of their adoption, became successful farmers and mechanics, and an important acquisition to the Queen's dominions.

The success of the Underground Railroad in transporting colored men to Canada presents a striking contrast with that of the African colonization scheme. The Colonization Society was organized in 1816—many years before the Underground Railroad was instituted. From the time of that organization to 1857, a period of forty years, there were

9,502 emigrants sent to Africa, of whom 3,676 were born free, 326 purchased their own liberty and 5,500 were emancipated on condition of being sent to Africa. It will thus be seen that nearly four times as many emigrated to Canada as to Liberia, and in developing the soil, building churches, schoolhouses, manufacturing establishments, and the surroundings of comfortable homes, and the facilities for the enjoyment of "life, liberty and the pursuit of happiness," the Wilberforce Colony will compare favorably with Liberia and Sierra Leone, though it is not doubted that African colonization has exerted a beneficial influence on the dark shores of the African continent. The Underground Railroad, it will be seen, has done much the greatest work in behalf of human liberty.

The conductors on this route were some of the noblest, self sacrificing men the world ever saw. No civil penalties dismayed them. They boldly proclaimed by deeds of moral heroism and self-sacrifice their faith in the higher law, before which human statutes were impotent when human liberty was at stake.

The remarkable exodus now in progress, which threatens to deprive the cotton States of a considerable portion of their laboring population, notwithstanding the sufferings of the refugees, presents a striking contrast with that under the management of the Underground Railroad. In the present case the philanthropist can exercise his charity toward the suffering, and no law can interfere with its penalties, while then, as will be seen by the sketches herewith presented, all acts of kindness to the fleeing fugitive, exposed those who aided them to the penalties of the fugitive slave law. The "higher law" has become practically national in its application to the colored people of the country.

The writer of the following sketches is well known throughout the region where the fugitives found their way to the Lakes, and was one of the most self-sacrificing and efficient of the conductors of the U. G. R. R. He is an earnest laborer for Him who "came to preach deliverance to the captive and to set at liberty those who are in bonds." In every good work for the benefit of humanity he has always borne a part when opportunity has offered.

The thrilling adventures narrated mostly occurred on his portion of the route, and within his personal knowledge. Many of the active participants in the service of the great line of travel from Slavery to Freedom, have already passed away. The author of these sketches is now in his 78th year, and can look back on a life of usefulness and good will to men far brighter than falls to the usual lot of mankind. The sketches were first published in serial numbers at the solicitation of the Editors of the Fredonia Censor, with a view to the perpetuation of the personal recollections of a period in our history which, thanks to the Proclamation of our martyred President, can never in the history of this country be repeated. Knowing so well the author, and the entire reliability of the narratives, and the deep interest which was taken in them when they were first given to the public, we have ventured to give them the permanent form in which they are now presented to the reader. They constitute an incomplete, but interesting record of "the times which tried men's souls." It was some ten years ago that these sketches were written. With others they are now presented to the public in a more enduring form, with the hope that the respect for the memory of those engaged in the self sacrificing work of befriending fugitives from slavery, may be more highly cherished. Surely when they shall "rest from their labors," and "their works shall follow them," they will be welcomed by Him who said, "Inasmuch as ye have done it unto the least of these *my brethren*, ye have done it unto me.

W. McK.

Fredonia, May, 1879.

PREFACE.

In 1619 slaves were introduced into the colony of Virginia—they were Africans of pure blood, jet black, thick lips, flat noses, flat feet and crooked shins. The Virginians would have scorned the idea of enslaving a white man or woman, but the time came when the bluest blood of Virginia betrayed itself in the blush on the cheek of beautiful women standing on the auction block in Richmond, Charleston and New Orleans. Beauty of face and of form had a market value; a beautiful woman would sell for the price of ten able bodied men, and even Christianity was an article of commerce. A man stands upon the block, dignified in manner, serious countenance, and silent. "Now, gentlemen and ladies," says the auctioneer, "I offer you a first class servant. He is honest and faithful, and moreover *he is a Christian*; no sham I tell you, but a genuine, conscientious Christian man. He would die rather than commit a wrong act or betray his master. How much do you offer for a servant that you can depend on every time?"

Good men in the Slave States were silent, having no means of redress; the laws and public opinion were on the side of the slave holder. The free States remonstrated and petitioned Congress to adopt measures for emancipation. The South assumed the political doctrine of State rights, which means that State laws are paramount to U. S. laws. But when the northern States enacted laws to 'protect their own citizens against kidnappers, it was found that "State Rights" applied only to slave States. As the free States persisted in protecting their citizens the slave States demanded the enactment of the Fugitive Slave Law, which was passed in 1850, establishing commissions and courts unknown to the Constitution, and was undoubtedly the most barbarous law enacted by any civilized nation in the 19th century.

The most simple act of charity to a fugitive must be kept a profound secret or a felon's cell was the penalty. The result was a spontaneous combination of multitudes of men and women, extending from Maine to Kansas, with many a station south of Mason & Dixon's line, which on account of its harmony of action, rapid transit and secret operation, came to be known as the "Underground Rail Road."

The Underground R. R., extending from the interior of the slave States to Canada, and to liberty, wherever human liberty could be found, had four main lines across the State of New York, and scores of laterals. It has finished its mission, closed its operations, settled its accounts and divided the proceeds among the *passengers*. The immense wealth thus accumulated was invested in the purchase of large tracts of land in Canada, clearing up, stocking and cultivating farms, building dwellings, barns, churches and school houses, mills and factories.

No institution has ever existed in this country, whose business was transacted with more perfect fidelity, more profound secrecy, more harmony in the working of its complicated machinery and yet with such tremendous results.

It had, like all other rail roads, its offices and stations, engineers and conductors, ticket agents and train dispatchers, hotels and eating houses. The fugitive slave law passed by Congress in 1850, imposed a penalty of $1,000 fine and imprisonment for selling or giving a meal of victuals to one of the passengers on this road, or for helping them on their way. Disregarding these penalties, the eating houses were open day and night, and well supplied with the best food the country afforded.

The business was conducted in silence and harmony, consequently but few of the employees suffered the aforesaid penalties; yet some of the noblest and purest men that ever suffered as martyrs were victims of that horrid fugitive slave law. Rev. John Rankin, of Ohio, was fined $1,000 and imprisonment. Wm. L. Chaplin, Esq., of Mass., was imprisoned in Virginia, released on nineteen thousand dollars bail, which was paid by his friends to save his life, and Rev. C. T. Torry died in a Virginia prison.

The managers availed themselves of all manner of facilities for traveling; rail roads and steam boats, canal boats and ferry boats, stage coaches, gentlemen's carriages and lumber wagons were pressed into active duty when needed. The large rivers were the chief obstacles in their way when not bridged with ice. In 1858 it was asserted that the slave holders had employed Douglass, (not Fred,) to advocate in Congress a bill to abolish the North Star and make it a penal offence for the Ohio river to freeze over. I do not think Douglass ever introduced such a bill, but such a proposition was no more absurd than the indirect attempt to abolish *Christianity*, by enacting the Fugitive Slave Law. The writer of these brief sketches of U. G. R. R. history kept a station and eating house at one of the crossings of the Cattaraugus river, in Cattaraugus Co., N. Y., though but few of his nearest neighbors knew until the rebellion ended, its usefulness. Being at the junction of six laterals with the main line running through Buffalo, I heard many thrilling accounts from escaping fugitives while they were in my charge, and experienced some exciting times when the slave hounds were almost within striking distance. I have given comparatively few of the many incidents which came under my observation, and these only in outline, yet as giving some conception of the workings of an institution importantly pertaining to a past epoch in our history, the character of which even now this generation can scarcely realize, I am persuaded that these chapters may have both value and interest, and they are therefore respectfully submitted in this form to the public.   E. M. Pettit. Fredonia, N. Y., May, 9.

CHAPTER I.THE SLAVE COFFLE AT WHEELING, VA.—THE KINDHEARTED LANDLORD—THE GOOD SAMARITAN—THE HUNTERS MISLED—THE ESCAPE.

Something over twenty years ago, I stopped a few days at the City Hotel in Wheeling, Va. The hotel was located on the southern border of the city, adjoining a small plantation in the rear of the garden. The landlord was a pleasant, social gentleman, well informed on all topics of interest, and preferred hiring his help rather than be the owner of a human being. Having learned this, I was less guarded in talking about their institutions than I should otherwise have been. Among the guests at the hotel was a family of Quakers on their way from Eastern Virginia to Indiana. One of the young men told me that he had never been outside of the State of Virginia; had long been disgusted with the wickedness and cruelty of slavery which he could not avoid seeing and hearing every day. The horrors of the everyday life on the plantations as described by him exceeded everything related in "Uncle Tom's Cabin," and he had sold out, and the family were going to settle in a free State. I was sitting on the piazza talking with this man, when a coffle slaves came in front of the house and were hustled along by the driver; the men were fine looking fellows, though they were bare-footed, and most of them bare-headed; they were chained by the right wrist to a long bar of iron. The women were not fettered, some of them carried infants in their arms, and some children rode on the wagon with the corn on which they all were fed. They soon started toward a steamboat lying at the levee, and were shipped for the New Orleans market. This was the first drove of slaves I had ever seen, and being a little excited, I made a remark to the Quaker which the landlord overheard, and touching my shoulder, he beckoned me to go with him. We went aside, and he said to me, "You are going to Kentucky, and I advise you to beware how you speak of these things. There are men in this place, who, had they heard that remark, would have had you in jail in a hurry. I hope you will heed my advice."

An incident that occurred on the U. G. R. R., not many months after, brought vividly to my remembrance the kind-hearted, unselfish landlord of the City Hotel in Wheeling. It was on a bitter cold day in December that a sleigh was driven into Fredonia, N. Y.; the driver had made some inquiries, (for this was his first trip as conductor,) and turned his team down the creek in search of a depot. It was late in the evening, and the road was badly drifted, but the train went through and made connection as usual. The passenger came out from under the driver's seat, shook off the blankets and Buffalo robes that had hid him and kept him warm. He was not inclined to talk at first, but a hearty welcome, a warm supper, and the assurance that he was safe from his pursuers, induced him to give a brief account of his adventures. He said: "I have always lived in Loudoun County, Virginia. My mother was the cook, and I worked about the house, and sometimes traveled with master,—went to Washington, Baltimore, Cumberland, and once to Wheeling, on horseback. One day, when mother gave me my dinner, she said, 'Charley, all my children gone but you, and Massa's done gone and sold you, and I'll never see you 'gin.' 'Guess not, mother, he promised you to keep me always;' but she said, 'I heard him tell the trader he'll send you to town Monday morning, and he must put you in jail.' Well, I was afraid to tell mother what I would do, because maybe somebody would hear, so I couldn't say good-bye to my poor old mother, but next morning master's best horse and I were 50 miles away towards Wheeling. Hid in the woods all day, at night left the horse loose in the woods and went on as well as I could. Did not go through the towns, went round, then found the road and went on. Found corn in the fields, and some apples, and got to Wheeling in about 14 or 15 days. Was almost starved, went into the City Hotel before daylight. The landlord was up, and I asked him for some bread. He looked at me and said, 'You are a runaway.' I began to say 'no,' but he said, 'Go with me!' We went to the barn, and he said, 'Do you know whose horse that is?' Then I owned up, and begged him to let me go and not tell master. He then read to me an advertisement, offering $500 reward for me. Then I thought, it's no use trying—must go back, sold! sold! Oh! I wanted to die; but the man said, 'See here! you see that house beyond that lot?' 'Yes, master,' I said. 'You go there and tell them I said they must take care of you, and give you something to eat.' Then he looked so happy, and I wanted to lie down and kiss his feet; but it was getting light. 'Hurry,' said he, "go right in the back door.' When I got in I could see nobody but a sick woman on a bed. I told what the man said, and soon I heard horses running up the road, and looking out, saw my master and another man coming. I began to cry, but she told me to get under the bed and lie still, and when I had done so she took up her baby, and got it to screaming with all its might. Soon master opened the door and looked in, and asked if a negro boy had come in there. The baby cried and she pretended to try to stop it, and asked him what he wanted. He repeated the question. She tried to hush the baby, and finally said, 'Husband is at the barn; he can tell you if he has been here.' They went to the barn, and soon I heard them running their horses up the road. Then she said to me, 'Go up the ladder and lie down on the floor,' which I did, and when the man came in with his milk pail, he asked his wife who that man was, inquiring about a boy? She said, 'I don't know, but I know where the boy is.' 'Where is he?' 'He went up the ladder, and you must carry him something to eat, poor fellow, he's starved.' As soon as he could, he came to me with enough to eat, and then fixed a place for me to lie down, and said, 'You are tired and sleepy. Now go to sleep, and if you wake, don't stir nor make a noise until I come.' Having slept little since I started, I slept all day; it was dark when he roused me up and told me to go down. I found a good supper ready, and while I was eating the man and his wife said not a word. When I had done he said, 'Come out here.' Following him, I saw at the door three horses; there was a man on one of them; I was told to mount one, and he mounted the other. I was between them. Not a word was spoken, and passing round the edge of the town near the hill, we came to the road leading north near the bluff above the river. I didn't know what it all meant, but supposed they were going to give me up, and claim the $500. We rode three miles maybe, hitched the horses in some bushes, and went down the steep bluff to the Ohio River. He pulled a stake and threw it into a boat that was tied to it, and motioned me to get in. We soon got across the river, then taking a little bundle, he directed me to go forward, and we were soon on a road. He then put two loaves of bread in my hand, and said to me, 'This is a free State, and there is the north star,' pointing to it; 'God bless you,' and I soon heard the splash of his pole in the river, and started northward."

Charley found himself alone in the road, the river on his right hand, broad fields on his left, and no house in sight; as to the north star, he looked towards it when his friend pointed towards it, but did not know which it was; his education had been neglected. Smart negroes knew that star by sight. When a slave could find the north star, and show his mother how he knew it, and by what signs he found it, he was ready to graduate—he had finished his education—but Charley, poor fellow, had been having an easy time, riding about with his master, caring for the horses, blacking his boots, and brushing his clothes, and had not thought of going north until his mother told him that he had been sold. Besides, Charley was terribly disappointed. He supposed he was to be delivered to his master; that a white man would feed him and help him on his way to freedom, when he could have $500 for less trouble and no risk, he had not supposed was possible. He began to feel dizzy and faint, went a few rods and sat down, and soon fell asleep. He dreamed that two men were putting him into jail; he struggled, and awoke up finding himself alone, and darkness all around. He soon aroused sufficiently to understand the situation, and started along the road, not knowing whether he was going north or south, but kept going until it began to be light, when he saw a paper nailed to a board fence with a picture of a negro running, and looking like the advertisement that the landlord showed him in his barn. While he stood looking at it, a man came behind him, put his hand on his shoulder, and said, what have we here? He turned to run, but the man held on to him, speaking kindly, and said, "don't be frightened, let us see what this is about;" then he read the advertisement, and looking at Charley, said, this means you; come with me, there is no time to be lost."He took him to a safe place far back in the woods, and seeing that he had bread with him, he said, "I will bring you more food to-night," and left him.

When he came to bring food, he told Charley that he would have to stay a few days until the men that were looking for him were gone. He was soon taken to a comfortable place, but it was two or three weeks before his kind conductor felt safe in starting with him.

The route from Wheeling was supposed to be towards Detroit at that season of the year, and the hunters were able to trace Charley going that way. They met, all along the way, men who had seen him, and could describe him as well as if they had known him from his childhood. Those rascally U. G. R. R. conductors were putting him through Carroll, Starke, Wayne, Ashland, and Huron counties, toward Detroit, where he could cross over. There were plenty of men along this route that were waiting to show them the way he had gone.

Meanwhile, Charley was on the short route to Buffalo, by way of Meadville, Pa., and Westfield, X. Y., *though no man saw him on the way.* At Westfield Mr. Knowlton kept the station, and it was his splendid team, that on that cold day in December, came into Fredonia and turned off at the old Pemberton stand on the West Hill, and landed Charley at the cosy little station in Cordova, from whence he was sent forward the next day to Black Rock and across the river to Canada.

In relating Charley's escape, I have met some people who doubted that story about the landlord in Wheeling. That kind of people have found the parable of the good Samaritan a stumbling block too great to get over, and so multitudes of men have neglected the whole of the New Testament rather than believe and practice its lesson.

CHAPTER II.DAN'S TRIP FROM DUNKIRK—SEES HIS MASTER IN THE CAR—R. R. CONDUCTOR'S ADVICE—FRIENDS IN NEED—SAFE ARRIVAL IN CANADA.

On a dark night in January, 1858, about midnight, we were aroused by heavy steps on the piazza, and the signal of the express train of the U. G. R. R. On opening the door we saw the laughing face of the conductor from the second station west, and above his head, (he was a short man,) the face of a terribly frightened negro. "Here," said the conductor, "is something to be done in a hurry; this is a valuable feller, I tell ye, and his master is close at his heels. You can't conceal him here, for the old man will be down on you before morning. He's a valuable feller, and they are sharp on his tracks."

We had a live engine in the barn, with a light car on runners, and the first impulse was to fire up and run to the next station, where friend Andrew and his good wife had a way of circumventing slave catchers in a manner peculiar to themselves, of which more may be said at another time. This plan was, however, rejected as unsafe.

On consultation it was decided that he should be lodged in an old house back in a field, on the skirts of the village, the house belonging to an old sailor, who had been converted from so-called Democracy to humanity, by having, while commanding a vessel on Lake Erie, been pressed into service in connection with the U. G. R. R. The Captain had been educated to believe in the so-called Democratic doctrine, "that slavery is the chief corner-stone of free institutions," but if I were to tell his experience in running his first train on this road, you would agree with me that the secrets of our officers would be safe in his hands. I may do so some time.

Dan had been forwarded from Corning to Dunkirk on a freight car, and on his arrival in the evening, the agent to whom he was consigned bought his ticket to Buffalo, and seated him behind the door at the rear end of the car. Just as it was starting two men came in and took seats near the other end of the car, their backs toward him. One of them was his master, and the other a celebrated slave hunter. When the conductor came for his ticket, Dan said to him, "Master, will you please stop and let me get off?" Conductor said, "are you afraid of those fellows with the red whiskers?" "Yes," said Dan, "I know 'em." "Do they know you are here?" "Guess not," said Dan. "Well, follow me, said the conductor. Taking Dan into another car, he told him to step off as soon as the train stopped, and go behind a woodpile, and the depot agent would find him as soon as the train started, and tell him where to go. The conductor told the agent, at Silver Creek, who found him as soon as the train started, so scared that he could hardly stand or speak, and sent a boy with him to a Democratic Deacon, Andrews, and he, without knowing it, put him again on the line of the U. G. R. R. in Arkwright, by giving him in charge of a colored man, John Little. The next night the wide-awake conductor, farmer Cranston, near Forestville, arrived at our station near 12 o'clock, as above stated.

Dan was warmed and fed, and secreted in the old house until it was deemed safe for him to go on, supposing the pursuers to have lost the track and abandoned the search. But not so; their spies were on the line watching every little skiff in Black Rock harbor, when friend Andrew, just at daylight, having signaled the boatmen, left his carriage in a back street, and led Dan through a narrow lane to where a boat lay hid, and out of the water. It was launched in a moment, and Dan and two boatmen were on their way to Canada before the spies watching the other boats could give the alarm.

While friend A. stood on the shore watching the fugitive as he landed on the Canada side, the slave hunters arrived on the spot, and seeing an honest looking face under a broad brim, inquired if he had seen a "nigger" starting from somewhere along there in a boat. Being answered in the affirmative, with a pretty good description of him, and the remark that "he is safe now, for he has just landed under the flag of Old England," they came out on the old man with a terrible volley of oaths, threats and imprecations. His cool answer was, "Friend, inasmuch as such conversation can avail thee nothing, would it not be wise to say no more about it? Farewell;" and he went to his carriage and started homeward.

Dan came back and worked for the Captain the next summer. Afterwards he attended school, and when the 112th Regiment went to the front, from this county, Dan went as waiter for an officer.

CHAPTER III. TOM STOWE HIS VALUE TO HIS MASTER—HIS BOY SOLD AND HIS WIFE DIES—HE FINDS HIS BOY—HIS ESCAPE TO PITTSBURG, AND THENCE TO CANADA.

The "fugitives from labor" who took passage on the U. G. R. R., were generally of the most intelligent class, and but for their use of certain words and phrases common to both master and servant in the slave States, they would often have been rejected as having no claim to accommodations on our line. One of the most remarkable men of this class that came this way was Tom Stowe. Tom's master was a sporting gentleman, living, when at home, on his plantation, about 18 miles from Vicksburgh, Miss., and was known from New Orleans to Baltimore as an enterprising, reckless and generally successful sporting man, but not as a common gambler. He kept from ten to twenty race horses, a half dozen fighting dogs, and never failed to buy the smartest fighting cocks, at whatever price. Tom said he had paid as high as $1,000 for a single cock. Tom was head man in his sporting establishment, managed the training, grooming, feeding and fitting of all the animals and birds, and had become so necessary and important an item in the concern, that Stowe more than once refused to sell him for $3,000, offered by rival sportsmen. They usually started north in April, by the way of the Mississippi and Ohio Rivers, sported some at Memphis, Louisville and Cincinnati, and leaving the steamboat at Wheeling, went up to Morgantown, where they stopped to recruit and fit the horses and fighting cocks for the June races and sporting in Baltimore. Stowe would often leave Tom in charge of the establishment while recruiting in Morgantown, and go to Philadelphia and Baltimore.

Morgantown is only six miles from the Pennsylvania line on the Monongahela River. The grocer of whom he bought supplies was in the habit of talking to him about the free States, and told him that he could get to Canada if he would try, but Tom answered that he had many times passed up the Ohio, and knew he was near the free States, but he did not wish to go away; besides, *his master could not spare him.* Tom had known this man four or five years, but was shy of him, supposing he intended to betray him for a reward, should he listen to his suggestions. After the races in Baltimore Tom was usually left in B. in charge of the stock, while Stowe went north to New York and Saratoga. In the fall, their sporting tour toward home was through Richmond, Charleston, Savannah and New Orleans. Thus by extensive travel and business intercourse with many men, Tom became intelligent, and carried about with him a heart-yearning for freedom. He was always well fed, well dressed, trusted with money, and left by his master often on the very borders of the free States. He remained faithful to his trust, and his master knew he would, and knew the reason why. Tom was, in size and form, a splendid specimen of a man; tall, straight, and handsome, nearly white, weighed about two hundred pounds, and not an ounce of spare material about him. Lucy, his wife, (as he described her,) was also nearly white, an octoroon, one of those whose rare beauty and accomplishments are the greatest misfortune that can befall one of her race. She had been brought up in the house, and was lady's maid to Stowe's wife. Stowe had consented to their marriage, hoping thereby to prevent Tom of availing himself of the U. G. R. R., in sight of whose depots along the Ohio River they often passed. They had a boy, who was the pride and joy of his mother. Stowe had bought some colts in Texas, and sent Tom to bring them home; and while he was absent the old man sold their little boy, only three years old, to a trader, in a paroxysm of rage because Lucy would not be unfaithful to Tom. When he came home, he found her but just alive, only able to tell him that Georgie had been sold to a trader by the name of Austin, and carried off. She died of a broken heart for the loss of her boy. It was difficult for Tom to get through this part of his story, and the meanest copperhead in our village, could he have heard and seen him, would never again dispute that a slave has a soul. After Tom had buried his wife, his first impulse was towards finding his boy, determined not to leave his master until he had learned something about him. Stowe avoided going north by their usual route, fearing, no doubt, that he would lose his man. At the end of two years Tom saw Austin, who told him that he sold Georgie to a lawyer in Savannah, and soon after, being in that city with his master, he called on the lawyer at his office, and asked him if he had bought such a boy. "Yes," he said, "I bought him, though I always was opposed to owning slaves, but they were selling the little fellow at auction. He would not have sold for $50 but for his beauty. They had bid $700; his beauty and his grief were too much for my caution and my principles, and on the spur of excitement, I bid $800, and no one would raise the bid. "Now," said he, "I suppose he must be related to you, as you are inquiring about him, and he looks like you." He directed Tom where to go, and said he would be home soon. When he called, he was invited into the parlor, where he found Georgie with his mistress, who had been teaching him to read. I cannot describe Tom's interview with his boy, and with the kind gentleman and lady with whom he was living. They would not regard him as a slave, and said if Tom should ever find himself in a condition to take care of Georgie, he should have him. I suppose Tom went for him with Gen. Sherman in his "March to the Sea," and that he found him in Savannah. If it were so, I wish I might have been there to see.

Tom's master never learned that he had found his boy, and as he had manifested no disposition to abscond, the old man went north again the next spring by the old route, stopping again at Morgantown to fit up for the sporting season. Stowe did not dare to leave Tom as formerly, but stayed there to keep an eye on him. Tom found his old friend, who advised him not to let this chance slip by without an effort to escape; he told him to cross over to the west side of the Monongahela River, keep along as, near the top of the mountain as possible to Pittsburgh, (describing the city so that he would know it,) go down the mountain so as to be at the bridge about dusk of the evening, cross over, passing through the city, cross over the Alleghany River, then go up that river, and it would bring him to Canada. "Well," said I, when Tom was telling his story, "The river does not reach all the way to Canada." "I found that out," said Tom, "but if I had not been picked up and put on to this route, I'd have followed that river as far as there was a drop of water in it." His friend gave him some bread, and Tom started and got on to the mountain—cut a heavy hickory cane, traveled in the day time and slept at night, never leaving the highest part of the mountain except when a ravine crossed his path, and arrived in sight of the city of Pittsburgh without having seen a man except once. The third day, about noon, he went down into a deep ravine, and came suddenly upon six men engaged in eating their dinner. One of them said, "There is that two thousand dollar nigger," and seizing an axe, came at him, ordering him to surrender. With the butt of his hickory cane Tom knocked the man down, when another man struck at him with an axe; stepping back, the axe missed him, and swung the man around so that Tom's bludgeon hit square across his mouth. He then ran up the ravine, and commenced climbing the almost perpendicular mountain, rolling a stone on to the only man that attempted to follow. The last he saw of the other three men, they were carrying off that man's body. Having learned by these men, as he supposed, that a reward of $2,000 was offered for him, he feared to go within speaking distance of any one, but managed to get through Pittsburgh, and followed along the rocky crest of the mountain within sight of the Alleghany River to near Franklin. Coming down near the road, he saw a negro coming towards him, and ventured to ask him to procure some bread for him, being nearly starved, and hardly able to walk with a sprain in his ankle. Tom's fear of being sent back was so great that he could hardly be persuaded to see the face of a white man. He supposed that everybody had seen the advertisement, and suspected even his negro brother. Tom was, however, in safe hands. His friend took him to our depot near Franklin, Pa., where he could not be induced to stay until his foot recovered, though it was much swollen, and he could bear no weight upon it. His route from Franklin came through Warren, Jamestown, Ellington and Leon. He asked me to put my name on his paper, on which I found the names of all the conductors that had put him through. He could not be persuaded to stay over but a day, therefore the train started at midnight, fording the river, and going through the dark woods, (a horrible road in those days,) arrived before daylight at Friend Andrew's hospitable station. Another idle day was passed, and the next morning about break of day, when Andrew put him on a boat at Black Rock, Tom sent his trusty hickory back to me. I had asked him for it, offering a nice cane in exchange, but he declined parting with it until he got beyond the force of the fugitive slave law; it had been his sole weapon, and in his strong arm had proved more than a match for six men, backed by a reward of $2,000.

I was so much interested by the following incident that I will relate it in Tom's own words. Tom was anxious to go to Cleveland, but dared not venture. A gentleman living there had offered to aid him should he ever need it, and he thought he would send for his boy if he could but see him. Tom said:

"Six years ago, we were coming north on a steamboat on the Mississippi, when the boat was burned. Mr. W., the gentleman above named, and his daughter, on his way home from New Orleans, occupied a state-room near the bow of the boat, where I had the horses. Master was frightened out of his wits, and begged me to save him, so I pushed the finest horse overboard, and got the old man into the river, with the tail of the horse in his hands; I then cut the lariat, and the horse landed the old man a mile below. The next thing I heard was a lady at her cabin window near by, screaming for help. I took her out of the window, threw the landing plank into the water, put her upon it, and by swimming with my hands on the plank, managed to land two or three miles down the river. Her father had left the cabin in search of means to save her, when the fire compelled her to accept my assistance, and she supposed he had perished; but he, having sought in vain for her, had been finally driven by the flames to the water, and by the aid of one of our horses, had got ashore. Each supposed the other had perished, but before noon he had found his daughter, and when he heard how she escaped, he offered Mr. Stowe any amount of money he should ask for my freedom; but the old man said that no money could induce him to part with me as long as he kept horses to be cared for. The lady gave me a diamond ring, for which a gentleman offered me $100, but it was on Lucy's finger when she died, and I buried it with her. I suppose it is there now."

In speaking of his own acts, Tom was very modest. His language was more like that of a Southern gentleman traveling in the North than I had ever heard from a slave before; but certain phrases were unmistakable. He was a genuine native of Mississippi.

This sketch is somewhat long, though I have omitted many interesting incidents related by Tom. I will add one laughable occurrence. A little before daylight one morning of Tom's flight, he looked into a cabin window, saw a table all set for breakfast, and the mistress sound asleep in a chair before the fire. No men were in sight, so Tom opened the door, seized a loaf of bread and a ball of butter and left. As he passed the old shanty barn, he heard the man, but he went on unmolested. Tom's description of the woman was ludicrous, and I always laugh when I try to imagine the consternation of those people when they sat down to that early breakfast.

CHAPTER IV.ORIGIN OF THE U. G. R. R.—"JO NORTON."

The first well established line of the U. G. R. R. had its southern terminus in Washington, D. C., and extended in a pretty direct route to Albany, N. Y., thence radiating in all directions to all the New England States, and to many parts of this State, Comparatively few crossed over to Canada until after the enactment of the fugitive slave law in 1850, at which time the aforesaid route had been in successful operation about eleven years. The severe penalties inflicted by that law for feeding, or aiding in the escape, or harboring "fugitives from labor," made it necessary to extend the lines of the R. R. directly through to Canada. Previous to 1850, slaves were sometimes seized and carried back under the Constitution, but no penalty could be inflicted for feeding, employing, or secreting them.

The General Superintendent resided in Albany. I know him well. He was once an active member of one of the churches in Fredonia. Mr. T., his agent in Washington city, was a very active and efficient man; the Superintendent at Albany was in daily communication by mail with him and other subordinate agents at all points along the line.

It should not be supposed that the few humble individuals actually engaged in the active operations of this institution, were the only persons interested in it. Some of the best men in the nation were stockholders; men of wealth and influence, men in office, State and national,—men, women and children identified themselves with its affairs. It had the aid and approval of the most distinguished philanthropists of the age, and many far-seeing politicians, descrying the conflict between slave and free labor, took sides with the latter.

It was a deep-laid scheme, having in view the restoration of God-given rights to helpless, hunted fugitives, making slaveholders realize that money paid for human chattels was an insecure investment, resulting in gradual emancipation, and finally in total abolition with the consent of the slaveholders themselves. Having thus slightly sketched the formation of the Company of the Underground R. R. and its object, I will narrate the wanderings of JO NORTON.

"UNDERGROUND RAILROAD—A MYSTERY NOT YET SOLVED."

Such was the heading of an article in one of the morning papers in the city of Washington, on Saturday morning of the last week in October, 1839, from which I copy as closely as I can from memory, not having time to look up the paper:

"The abolition incendiaries are undermining, not only our domestic institutions, but the very foundations of our Capitol. Our citizens will recollect that the boy Jim, who was arrested while lurking about the Capitol in August, would disclose nothing until he was subjected to torture by screwing his fingers in a blacksmith's vice, when he acknowledged that he was to have been sent north by railroad; was to have started from near the place where he stood when discovered by the patrol. He refused to tell who was to aid him—said he did not know—and most likely he did not know. Nothing more could be got from him until they gave the screw another turn, when he said, *the railroad went underground all the way to Boston.*" Our citizens are losing all their best servants. Some secret, Yankee arrangement has been contrived by which they "stampede" from three to eight at a time, and not a trace of them can be found until they reach the interior of New York, or of the New England States. They cannot gave gone by railroad, as every station is closely watched by a secret police, yet there is no other conveyance by which a man can reach Albany from this city in two days. That they have done so, is now fully demonstrated. Colonel Hardy, a tobacco planter, residing in the District, about five miles from the city, lost five more slaves last Sunday evening. They were pursued by an expert slave catcher, but no trace of them was discovered. The search was abandoned this morning, the Colonel having received a paper called the *Liberty Press*, printed in Albany, with an article marked, so as to attract his attention, which reads as follows:

"'ARRIVED, this morning, by our fast line, three men and two women. They were claimed as slaves by Colonel H., of the District of Columbia, but became dissatisfied with the Colonel's ways, and left the old fellow's premises last Sunday evening, arriving at our station by the quickest passage on record.'

"The article goes on reciting certain incidents that have transpired in the Colonel's family, that correspond so exactly with facts that the Colonel says, 'Nobody but Kate could have told that story! 'Said article closes by saying: 'Now, Colonel H., please give yourself no trouble about these friends of yours, for they will be safe under the protection of the British Lion before this meets your eyes.'"

Thus it will be seen that this famous thoroughfare was first called the "Underground Railroad," in the city of Washington.

That article was published in the Liberty Press for "a southern market." The facts of the case are these: The three men, Jo, Robert, and Harry, lay concealed in a rude cabin, which was covered out of sight by a pile of corn stalks, about six miles from Baltimore, near the road toward Washington. The women, Kate and Nancy, were in a similar hut near by during the first day, but were conveyed in a carriage to a safe place in Baltimore, Monday evening, arriving there about eight o'clock. These were the first two stations on the route, and here they all remained until the aforesaid article appeared in the Washington paper, and Col. H. had called in his hounds, both biped and quadruped, when, the excitement having subsided, their further progress was comparatively easy.

Before pursuing the thread of their story beyond this point, I must go back a few days and commence the narrative as it was related at my own fireside by one of the parties, the aforesaid Jo, whom I chanced to meet in this village and made a bargain with to go to school, paying for his board by doing chores. Jo was very intelligent, but said his uncle Harry was a "heap" smarter than he was, and led the party whenever they ran their own train.

Jo worked on the plantation "making tobacco," as he termed it, in the summer, and after he was sixteen years old, he was hired out as waiter in a hotel in Washington every winter. He used to boast of standing behind Daniel Webster's chair, and waiting on him at the table, and that his wife, Mary, had the care of his rooms. They had now been married about four years. She lived, when not in service at the hotel, with the Judson family in the city. Judson held her as a slave, though his father told her, that by his will, she would, at his death, be free. When Jo was not employed in the city, he was allowed to go to church, and to visit his wife on Sunday once in two weeks. When the gout got an extra twist on the old Colonel's toes, he would be cross and refuse to give him a pass. But Jo had a true friend in the old man's daughter, whose love letters he carried both ways, and never betrayed her secrets. She did the old man's writing at such times, and would always provide him with a pass without asking very carefully whether it was his day to go to town or not.

Jo had long meditated an escape, more for the sake of Mary, and for the anxiety they both felt for their little boy, James, than on his own account. On his way home one Sunday evening, he fell in company with a gentleman walking in the same direction. Jo knew by his language that he was from the north, and felt, (as he expressed it,) in his bones, that the gentleman might be trusted as a friend. I need not relate all that passed between them; another interview was appointed at the end of two weeks, at which time it was arranged that Mary and the little boy should remain a while longer, and Jo was to start with some others, three weeks from that evening.

Just after it was dark, at the time appointed, at the signal, Jo slowly raised his head above a clump of bushes in which he was concealed, in the old cemetery by the turnpike, near the bounds of the city, and was astonished to see four other heads arise as if they came out of the graves, from behind tombstones and low bushes; all of them silent and motionless, until they heard signal No. 2, when, with silent tread, they all approached the signal station, trembling with superstitious fear, without even daring to whistle to keep off the "spooks." When they came together, all of them were surprised to find that they were acquainted and related to each other.

Each knew that others were going, but none knew who the others were until they met among the tombs. The other four had been hired out by Colonel H. to different parties in the city, and not one had revealed to any other the secret of their movements. The man who met them there was a stranger to all of them, as they expected he would be, but having exchanged signals they confided in him. Jo always declared that they were expecting to "just go down into the ground among the dead folks," and in some mysterious way be carried off, and their fears had almost got the better of their longings for liberty, when they were joyfully relieved by the conductor, who told them that they were to follow the turnpike until they came near the railroad, then "take the R. R. track, passing around stations in the fields and woods, find the track again, and go on until you see a man standing in the middle of the track; then stop and listen, and if you hear him say 'Ben,' go to him and do as he tells you." He then appointed Harry as their conductor, told them to walk fast, as they had thirty miles to go, showed them the north star and its bearings upon their route, shook hands, and with quivering lips, bade them God speed. They were soon out of his sight.

They traveled by starlight until about midnight, when clouds obscured the stars, and in passing around a village, they got bewildered and lost. After wandering in the fields and woods an hour or more, they stopped to consult about their course, and found that there were five different directions, each of which was strenuously contended for as the way to go, and there would probably have been six ways had there been another man in their party. They were almost in despair when the clouds broke away, and Harry said, "Now I find him." Harry's education consisted of one lesson in astronomy, viz.: how to find the north star by the bearing of the constellation called the "great bear." Harry soon discovered it, and said in low tones, "dis am de way, know it all de time, dat am de old norf," pointing at the star. It happened, however, to be Kate instead of Harry, that had guessed right. So much time had been lost, that, as Jo said, "de chickens began to crow" before they discovered "Ben" standing on the track. They stopped until Ben spoke his own name, when they followed him into a field, and coming to a stack of corn stalks, Ben removed a few bundles, and the men went in. The women were secreted in a similar place, and after a hearty breakfast, provided for them by their host, they all laid down and slept soundly.

Ben was a free negro, very old and decrepit. He had been supplied with money to rent this field, and "make a crop of corn," and to fix up the place and take care of it. The stacks of corn in which they were secreted were close to the railroad, so that no one would look in so public a place for fugitives. Old Ben, during the next day, obliterated all tracks in the field by husking and moving his bundles of stalks. As soon as it was dark a man took Kate and Nancy away. They walked along the track to a cross road, and along the road some distance, then started for Baltimore in a coach, driven by a negro. The boys did not awake until an hour after the women were gone, when they were aroused by a pack of hounds. The dogs were moving carefully about, as they often do when the track is old, occasionally giving out a sharp yelp. When they struck the fresh tracks of Kate and Nancy, who had been gone about an hour, the whole pack broke into a wild scream, varying between the hoarse howl of the old hounds and shrill screech of the pups.

CHAPTER V. JO NORTON, CONTINUED MAKING THEIR WAY FROM WASHINGTON TO ALBANY JO GOES TO SCHOOL LECTURES TO BUY HIS WIFE AND CHILD SUCCEEDS THE HAPPY MEETING.

The plan adopted by the enterprising managers of the U. G. R. R. to mislead the owners of the fugitives, and induce them to give up the chase, was kept secret a long time, and great numbers escaped thereby without capture or accident between the Capitol city of the Nation to that of our own State. A letter containing an account of the flight of a party, with sufficient details to enable the manager at Albany to get up a "local article" for the *Liberty Press*, was sent by mail as soon as they left Washington.

The boys did not leave the station kept by Ben, nor the girls their hiding-place in Baltimore, until the owner had abandoned the pursuit, having learned by the aforesaid paper, *what he took as positive proof*, that they were beyond his reach.

There were many exciting incidents related by Jo, in connection with their passage north, but the space allotted to these sketches will not admit of their relation. I will briefly say that the boys passed through the city of Baltimore between eight and nine o'clock in the evening, passing through the most public streets, stopping two or three times to buy apples and peanuts at the fruit stands, for which purpose their guide and conductor had given them some money. He (the guide), was a sharp colored boy, not more than thirteen years old. They followed their instructions, by keeping in sight of their guide, and talking about a meeting which had been held that evening, from which they appeared to be returning home. As Jo and Harry were zealous Methodists, it was easy for them to prolong a conversation on such a topic indefinitely; "the powerful preach-in," and "how happy that yaller gal was," &c., they talked as loudly and as earnestly as others, who, at that hour, crowded the well-lighted streets. They reached the outskirts of the city before the hour when negroes must not be seen in the streets, where they met the girls in charge of a man, who gave further directions, and started north. From thence to Philadelphia they traveled on foot in the night, stopping through the day at farm houses with Quakers. Jo said they never failed to find a good breakfast in readiness on their arrival, and the people expecting them before it was light.

From Philadelphia they went on a small fishing boat to Bordentown, thence to New York by railroad. The boys were stowed away among bales and boxes in a freight car, and the girls by the evening train in a first-class car; they were dressed as ladies, with veils over their faces. A gentleman, assuming the air of a Southerner, walked between them, pushing aside a man at the door, whose business it was to detect runaway slaves; they stepped in just as the car started. Having arrived safely in New York, they were pushed forward to Albany, and Jo's companions being provided for, we dismiss them and follow only the fortunes of Jo.

Jo was expecting that his wife, Mary, and their little boy, would come on by a route better suited to their condition, but he soon heard that her master, having detected her in an attempt (as he supposed), to get away, threw her into prison until he could sell her to be sent into the rice swamps; the worst punishment that could be inflicted on a slave. This was a terrible blow to Jo's prospects, and having saved a few dollars by his industry, he left his friends in Albany, and started west under instructions just a year from the day he left the old plantation. He wanted to find a place where he could work for his board and go to school. I kept him on such terms, and he began to learn the alphabet at twenty-five years of age. He was faithful and attentive to his business and his books, and although naturally overflowing with mirth and music, he had frequent attacks of deep melancholy, amounting to almost despair, on account of the uncertainty of the fate of his wife and child.

Soon after Congress met in December, 1840, I learned that General Chaplin was in Washington reporting for his paper, the aforesaid Liberty Press, of which he was one of the editors, and I proposed to Jo to ask him to enquire after Mary, to which he assented, though with but little hope of success. But as soon as the letter, giving Mr. C. directions to guide him in looking for Mary, was mailed, Jo became very nervous, called at the post office two or three times a day, and began to wonder that the letter had not been answered before it could have reached Washington. In eight or ten days the answer came. Mr. Chaplin had found Mary living with Mr. Judson her old master. She had been in the jail three months during which time another child was born and had died. Judson then proposed to forgive her, and take her again into his family on condition she would solemnly promise to never again attempt to run away, to which she agreed, and gave up all hope of ever seeing her husband. He told Mr. C. that he had just been offered $800 for her, but she was a favorite servant in his family; moreover, he had never sold a slave, and thought he never would, but if her husband wished to redeem her and her boy, now four years of age, he would accept for both $350, if paid by March 4th, at which time Mr. C. would go home, and could take them along, provided the money could be raised. Jo laughed and cried, prayed and gave thanks to the blessed Lord all at once, but soon fell again into despair, for how could he get so much money in so short a time?

It was arranged that Jo should undertake to raise the money himself by holding meetings in school-houses in country districts, tell his own story, relate incidents in plantation life, &c., and take up collections. Accordingly, appointments were sent to nearly all the schools in the town, and in two days the work was begun. Jo went to school every day, and at night he would go from two to six miles and hold a meeting. At the first meeting we collected $6, a good beginning for a country district. After some ten days he gave up his school, and taking letters to leading abolitionists in adjacent towns, he started off alone. On the 26th day of January, I met him by appointment at Ellicottville. I had, the day before, received another letter from Mr. Chaplin, containing an offer from Judson, to take $50 less than his first offer, provided the $300 should be paid him by the first day of February. On counting his money it amounted to only about $100; several gentlemen, came into Esquire H——'s office, where we were, and Judge Chamberlain, now deceased, proposed to be one of ten men who were present, to give a joint note for $200, and all share alike in paying the balance after Jo had done all he could before his wife should arrive. The note was made, and T. R. Colman, of Dunkirk, a gentleman who is now a successful banker in Chautauqua County, advanced the money, being himself one of the signers of the note, and one of the lawyers of Ellicottville drove to Buffalo, fifty miles, in a terrible storm, bought a draft and mailed it in time to reach Washington by the date specified, so that free papers were secured for Mary and her boy.

It was agreed that Jo should send money as fast as collected to Mr. E. Shepard Colman, of Ellicottville, and if there was not enough to pay the note, he was to collect the balance from the signers and pay it. Jo then started on a "lecturing tour," as he called it, through Wyoming, Genesee and Erie Counties, collecting small sums wherever his friends could get up a meeting, and when he arrived at my house again on the 10th day of March, I had just received a letter from Mr. Chaplin, saying that he had brought Mary and her boy to Utica, and Jo must come without delay. He gave me every dollar that he "had collected, which was only about $5 short of the amount due on the note; I gave him $30 of it, and he started for Utica about sunset; although he had walked from Buffalo that day, 27 miles, he walked back in time to take an early train the next morning. A few days after, I met an old friend who resided in

Syracuse, who told me that he met Jo on the train, and learning from him his story, he went to Utica with him, intending to witness the meeting, but was not present when they first met each other; however, he was well paid for going by witnessing their happiness soon after. In due time I received a line from Mr. C., of Ellicottville, acknowledging the receipt of the money, and as it fell short but $35, he had paid the whole of the note, and said, "you and I will make all right between us." However, as it turned out, there was nothing left to be made right between us, for in a few months he received a letter containing a draft for the $35; he could not decipher much of the letter, but the signature, "Jo Norton," was sufficiently legible to explain it all.

CHAPTER VI."JO NORTON," CONTINUED—HIS QUICKNESS AT REPARTEE LECTURES IN VILLENOVA—SETTLES IN SYRACUSE—ENFORCING THE FUGITIVE SLAVE LAW—THE "SHADRACH" CASE IN BOSTON—EFFECT ON SYRACUSE AND THE EMPIRE STATE.

I have given in detail facts and incidents as evidence of Jo Norton's industry, thrift and honesty. He was a serious, devoted Christian, yet his wit and mirthfulness were often exhibited in keen repartee, and sarcastic answers to persons who sought opportunity to embarrass him while speaking. There were, even then, men of copperhead proclivities, some of whom would occasionally interrupt him, but I never knew one to try it the second time. He was once asked if he worked hard when he was a slave? "No!" he replied, "I didn't work hard when I could help it." "Did you have enough to eat?"

"Yes, such as it was."

"Did you have, decent clothes?"

"Yes, midlin'."

"Well," said the fellow, "you were better off than most people are here, and you were a fool to run away."

"Well, now," said Jo, "the place that I left is there yet, I suppose, guess nobody's ever got into it, and if my friend here wants it, he can have it by asking for it, though perhaps he had better get his *Member of Congress to recommend him.*"

Another fellow asked, "Is the speaker in favor of amalgamation?"

" 'Gamation? what's that?"

"It means blacks and whites marrying together."

"Oh, that's it! as for such things, they depend mostly upon people's taste. For my part, I have a colored woman for my wife,—that's my choice—and if my friend here wants a black wife, and if she is pleased with him, I am sure I shan't get mad about it."

Soon after he commenced collecting funds to redeem his family from bondage, he was invited to go to a school-house in Villenova. He went alone, on foot; when near the place, he saw two boys chopping, and heard one of them say, "There's the nigger." Jo stopped and said, "I ain't a nigger! I allus pays my honest debts; my master was a nigger! See here!" said Jo, "when you chop, you be a chopper, isn't that so?" "Yes." "Well, when a man *nigs*, I call him a *nigger*. Now, my old master, he nigged me out of all I ever earned in my life. Of course, he is a nigger!" and Jo sang the chorus of one of Geo. W. Clark's Liberty songs:

> "They worked me all de day,
> Widont one cent of pay;
> "So I took my flight
> In de middle ob de night,
> When de moon am gone away."

"Now, boys, come over to the school-house this evening, and I'll sing the rest of it." That evening Jo had a full house and a good donation.

Jo removed to Syracuse, bought a lot, built a good house, was doing a thriving business and accumulating property when the "fugitive slave law" was passed, and the business of catching and returning fugitives from bondage became very active, under the auspices of our second "accidental chief magistrate," who signed the bill, and then enforced it with all the influence and patronage he could command. I have now before me his proclamation, calling on the army and navy to rally to the aid of the blood-hounds in running down a poor man in Boston, by the name of "Shadrach."

Shadrach had escaped from the "fiery furnace" of slavery. The U. S. Marshal seized him, and was binding him hand and foot for the purpose of "pitching him in" again, but the cords that bound him, somehow came apart, and Shadrach walked away, and this time there was not even the smell of the aforesaid fire on his garments. This put new energy into Mil—rd, he sent a special message to Congress, then in session, urging them to pass more stringent laws, so that he could compel his "subjects" to fall down and worship the image that he had set up. Shadrach was re-captured, taken in a man-of-war to Richmond, and sold at auction, his purchaser giving bail that he should be sent south of Virginia. In 1864 I saw a notice in the papers that he had returned to Boston. The fire of slavery had not consumed him, but the fire on Fort Sumter had severed the cords that bound him.

The story of "the Shadrach case in Boston" made the city of Syracuse a hot-bed-of abolitionism. The people met in convention, denounced the law and the men who enacted it, and resolved that no slave should be carried out of Syracuse. The slaveholders, encouraged by the course pursued by the President and the leading members of Congress of all parties, became more and more insolent, and cracked their slave whips in plantation style. One of them threatened on the floor of Congress, that whenever another anti-slavery convention should be held in Syracuse a fugitive should be arrested and sent back to slavery from that city. The Empire State held a Convention at Syracuse soon after, and an attempt was made to execute that threat, but Syracuse stood firm to her resolutions, and the attempt failed; but the "Jerry rescue" shook the State from center to circumference. Jo was in that melee

CHAPTER VII. THE "JERRY RESCUE"—JO NORTON HEADS THE PARTY THAT RESCUES JERRY—EXCITING TIMES IN SYRACUSE—THE FUGITIVE SLAVE LAW IN CONTEMPT—JO GOES TO CANADA.

The fugitive slave, named Jerry, had been discovered by a detective employed by his master, a month or two previous to the Anti-Slavery Convention, which had been announced for the first of August, I think, though I am not certain as to the exact time, and the agent of the claimant had been several weeks making arrangements to carry out the programme that was announced in Congress, and published and repeated by the press all over the South. "That hot-bed of Abolitionism had got to be humbled; Syracuse was to be taught that there was a State known as 'Old Virginia,' 'The Old Dominion,' 'Mother of Presidents,' " though even Virginia rejoiced in being able to shirk the responsibility of having brought into the world the accidental tenant of the White House, whom the chivalry were employing to do their dirty work.

I met Jo early in the morning on the day of the convention. He said that many of the fugitives had left for Canada, having heard rumors that one or more of them were to be arrested on that day, but, said Jo, "I have a pleasant home here, my children are going to school, and I have all the work I can do. Besides all that," said he, "there are not men enough in Virginia to carry me out of this city. If there is to be any excitement of that sort here, I'm bound to have a hand in it, and I shall stay and help fight it out."

The vague rumors that were afloat were not sufficient to put Jerry and his friends upon their guard. The only persons who knew what was going on were such as sympathized with the slaveholder, for animals of the "genus copperhead," had already become sufficiently numerous to

consume a vast amount of bad whiskey. A marshal was brought from
Rochester to make the arrest, for no citizen of Syracuse could be found
who dared to "face the music." Jerry, all unconscious of danger, was
busily employed, hammering away at a barrel in a cooper shop, when
about twelve o'clock he was seized, and, after a brave fight, was ironed
hand and foot, thrown upon a cart that the marshal had pressed into
his service, and started for the office of the Commissioners.

The Convention had organized in Market Hall, and commenced
business, when a man came in and interrupted the proceedings by
saying, in an excited manner, "Mr. President, an officer from Rochester
has arrested a fugitive, and is now carrying him off; they are now on the
canal bridge." In a moment the Convention was broken up, men,
women, and children rushed into the street, and ran toward the bridge,
but before the crowd arrived the marshal had got Jerry into the
Commissioners' office.

The city was in an uproar; no such excitement had ever been witnessed
in Syracuse before. Thousands of people from the country and adjacent
towns were there to attend the Convention. The fugitives and free
colored men surrounded the building, and they were surrounded on all
sides by a dense mass of people. Some of the best lawyers in the State
were present, and volunteered their services to defend Jerry, while one
lawyer sold his services to the slave catchers. The Commissioners' office
was on the second floor of a large brick building, one side of which
fronted on the canal. The outside door was fastened with heavy bars,
and the inner door securely locked to keep out the crowd, and it was
with difficulty that Jerry's friends and counsel got into the room where
the trial was to be held.

The trial was protracted and delayed until the court and counsel were
tired out and hungry, and adjourned for supper, leaving the prisoner in
charge of the marshal and his deputies. The officer took pains to make
the crowd understand that he was armed, and would shoot down any

man who should attempt to rescue the prisoner. Meanwhile, Jo had organized a party, and had everything ready to storm the stronghold of the slave power in Syracuse. Although it was time to light the lamps in the streets, the crowd had not diminished nor the excitement abated. The court and counsel had but just reached the hotel when Jo gave the signal to his men, and in an instant a stick of timber twenty feet long was mounted on the shoulders of as many stout negroes as could stand under it; at the word "Jo," with a shout and run, the battering ram was thrown upon the door, and carried all before it. Then Jo, at the head of his men, with a crow-bar in his hands, ran up stairs and attacked the inner door. The marshal was a brave man for so great a rascal,—none but rascals of a high grade would accept Fillmore's commission under the fugitive slave law—and when the door gave way under the furious blows of Jo's crow-bar, he fired at him, but Jo was too quick for him. The ball went into the floor, and the marshal's arm hung limp at his side, shattered by the crow-bar. The men rushed in and seized the deputies but the marshal jumped through an open window, and fell thirteen feet to the tow-path of the canal; he managed to get away in the shadow of the building, and found his way to a surgeon's office. Jerry was found lying on the floor, bloody, almost naked, and bound in chains. He had proved himself a hero by fighting the whole United States in the persons of the President's special Commissioners. He was provided with clothes and money, and the poor fellow never saw the city of Syracuse again by daylight. The next time we heard from him he was making barrels in Canada.

J. W. Loguen, (colored,) and several others, were equally active with Jo Norton in the Jerry rescue, but Jo was enthusiastic, brave and unselfish, strong, and nimble as a cat, and no one doubted his ability to lead in such an affray. The natural kindness of his disposition would lead him to prefer breaking the marshal's arm to save his own life, rather than to break his head. Rev. J. W. Loguen, and several others, were arrested and taken to Albany, where they were tried for rescuing the slave, but the jury failed to agree upon a verdict. They were then sent for trial to Canandaigua, with the same result, and the prosecution was finally abandoned. For more than a year the Jerry rescue trials kept the State in great excitement, but no verdict was obtained against any one The Fugitive Slave Law was brought into contempt, and Northern dough-faces were taught a salutary lesson.

Joe could not be made to believe that it was possible to carry him out of Syracuse as a fugitive, but he might be taken to Albany or elsewhere to be tried for the part he had taken in behalf of Jerry, and away from his friends he would be liable to be arrested and carried back to slavery, for Col. H. had long known where he was. Therefore he concluded to sell his property and go to Canada. He settled in Toronto, where he was respected as a citizen, and took a great interest in the education of his family, and in promoting the best interests of fugitives who were constantly arriving there.

The operations of the Underground Railroad were not suspended nor in the least disturbed by the efforts of the President to enforce the fugitive slave law in Syracuse, in illustration of which fact I quote from a Syracuse paper soon after, the following card:

"TO THE FRIENDS OF THE FUGITIVES FROM SLAVERY."

"The members of the Fugitive Aid Society find it no longer convenient nor necessary to keep up their organization. The labor of sheltering those who flee from tyranny, providing for their immediate wants, and helping them to find safe homes in this country and in Canada, must needs devolve, as it always has devolved, upon a very few individuals. Hitherto, since 1850, it has been done, for the most part, by Rev. J. W. Loguen. He, having been a slave and a fugitive himself, knows best how to provide for that class of sufferers, and to guard against imposition. Mr. Loguen has agreed to devote himself wholly to this humane work, and to depend for the support of himself and family, as well as the maintenance of this depot on the Underground Railroad, upon what the benevolent and friendly may give.

We, therefore, hereby request that all fugitives from slavery, coming this way, may be directed to him; and that all clothing or provisions contributed may be sent to his house, or such places as he may designate.

Mr. Loguen will make semi-annual reports of his receipts of money, clothes or provisions, and of the number of fugitives taken care of and provided for by him, and he will submit his accounts at any time to the inspection of any persons who are interested in the success of the Underground Railroad.

SAMUEL J. MAY,
JAMES FULLER,
JOSEPH A. ALLEN,
LUCIUS J. COMSBEE,
WILLIAM E. ABBOTT,
HOSEA B. KNIGHT.

That notice only affected the line through Syracuse. I have made the quotation from a paper now before me, that the readers of these brief sketches may understand that the U. G. R. R., about which so much has been said and so little was known, was no myth, and that its operations became more public and more successful after than they were before the passage of the fugitive slave law.

CHAPTER VIII.GEORGE AND CLARA—THEY REACH OBERLIN—HOTLY PURSUED—TAKE PASSAGE WITH CAPT. TITUS—RECOGNIZED BY THEIR OWNER—CAPT. TITUS' EXPERIENCE—AN INCIDENT OF THE BURNING OF THE ERIE—ESCAPE OF THE FUGITIVES.

Among the exciting incidents connected with the U. G. R. R., no case excited our sympathy more than that of George and Clara. George had been his young master's body servant; was of medium height and fine proportions, intelligent, respectful, and uncommonly efficient in business. Clara was his sister; she had been lady's maid, and had never been overtasked with hard work. Both of them had seen a good deal of polite society, and availed themselves of such advantages as came in their way to acquire information, and some of the rudiments of an education. They were polite and respectful in their manners, and were as contented and happy as people in their condition could be, and perhaps they would have remained in slavery, rather than run the risk of the terrible punishment they knew awaited them, if they should be captured, had not her master sold Clara to a trader, who boasted that he could sell her in New Orleans for $3,000. His excuse for selling hers when his family remonstrated, was that she was insolent and refused to obey him. The usual remedy for such fault having failed, he sold her; the particular thing in which she disobeyed he said little about,—whatever it was, *it had not reduced her market value.*

A peculiar affection had always existed between the brother and sister. Few slaves had as many comforts and advantages as George, yet he loved his sister more than all other things, and when he heard that she was sold, and her probable fate, he decided at once to save her or die in the attempt. Having traveled with his master, he knew the roads, and what was of more importance, he knew many slaves in most of the towns along their route.

From the time they started from near the capitol of Kentucky, until they arrived at Oberlin, a noted U. G. R. R. station, within a few miles of Lake Erie, was many weeks, yet there was hardly an hour in which they were not in imminent danger of being captured. Major Curtis, their master, employed Bill Shea, the most noted slave catcher in the State, to aid in capturing them, but George managed to throw the dogs off the track. They went southeast, then turning northeast they got into the mountains, and after four weeks they crossed the Ohio River, near Parkersburgh, in West Virginia. Our enterprising conductor near that town had them in charge before they crossed over. The pursuit was so hot and well conducted, that although their track had been often lost, it had been as often recovered, and the conductors were many times driven to their wit's end in eluding the pursuers. When they arrived at the aforesaid station, they were safe for the time; they might stay there, for they were well secreted, besides, slave-hunters themselves were not in a safe place if found prowling about Oberlin College.

Curtis was determined to capture them at all hazards. He employed spies at different points along the line, and at all the Lake ports from Cleveland all the way to Buffalo. He stayed at Cleveland, but Bill was setting his traps along the line. As soon as it was supposed that the pursuit had been abandoned, George and Clara were started east along the line, with a sharp look-out ahead. The spies had been outwitted, and the fugitives had passed this point, when a dispatch came along the line (not by telegraph, no wires had then been put up), *that all the crossings at Buffalo, Black Rock and Niagara Falls, were unsafe.*

They were then hidden away until an opportunity offered to smuggle them, in disguise, on to a steamboat at her first stopping place on her way from Buffalo to Detroit. When the boat came to the dock it was 10 o'clock in the evening, and when the crew commenced "wooding up," two new hands, dressed as sailors, came from among the wood piles, and though somewhat awkward, they worked with all their might, and when the wood was all loaded, they went aboard with the sailors, and were soon on their way.

Meanwhile, Bill Shea, Curtis' accomplice, having been baffled, had returned to Cleveland to consult with Curtis. They decided to abandon the pursuit, and take the first boat for Sandusky, thence by stage to Cincinnati. The boat on which our fugitives had taken passage was one of the finest side-wheel steamers on the lake, commanded by Captain Titus, a very popular captain, and the same who was in command of the Erie when she was burned off Silver Creek. The boat stopped at Cleveland for passengers, and just as she was starting off, Curtis and Bill came running and jumped on board. When they called at the office to pay their passage to Sandusky, the clerk said, "We do not stop there, we run to Detroit direct." "Well, Major," said Bill, "we are in for it, I guess it's your treat," and they passed down toward the bar. Bill could never pass anybody without looking to see if they answered the description of some slave advertisement of which he had his hat full. In pursuit of this laudable object, he stopped to look at two individuals dressed in sailor costume, seated among the bales of freight. At the first glance he knew his man. Stepping back, he seized the Major and turned him about, saying, "There he is; Major, if that isn't George, may I never see Lize again or have a nibble at her corn dodgers." Curtis looked at them, recognized both, and said, "Bill, the other one is the girl, dressed up in sailor toggery." By this time the fugitives had seen and recognized their pursuers, and were so agitated that they could not utter a syllable. Curtis walked up to them and said, "How do ye do? got into business, ha? how do you like it? wasn't aware that you understood this business. Clara could do better with women's clothes on. Come, go with me, I'll introduce you to the captain; it would be the making of this boat to have you in the ladies' cabin. I should think by your appearance that you are sick of the business, and maybe you would like to go home; if so, you can go with us, as we are going right back. How lucky for you that we happened to meet." The talk was embellished with horrid oaths, and continued a long time without a word in answer from the frightened fugitives.

Captain Titus happened to be passing, and stopped to witness the scene. He had seen and heard it all. When Curtis saw him he said, "Well, captain, I am in luck this time! Here I have been chasing these slaves of mine up and down this Lake shore about a month, and finally lost track of them and started for home. Bill and I have, I fear, committed a sin in swearing about getting on the wrong boat, and now it appears that a kind Providence has directed our steps all the time without our asking. How long have they been in your employ? One of them is a girl! didn't you know it? "When he stopped and gave a chance to answer, the Captain said, "I know nothing about it. I saw them here this morning, and suppose they came aboard somewhere last night." "All right," said Curtis, "and Captain, I want you to do me a favor. You go to Detroit, I believe." "Yes," said the Captain. "Well, if you will stop your boat at a convenient place in Detroit River, and let us ashore, I will give you a hundred dollars. The city of Detroit is a very unsafe place in which to handle this kind of property." "Very well," said the Captain, "I will land at any place you choose, and will charge you nothing for it." "Thank you," said Curtis, "but I shall pay you well for the favor."

Captain Titus turned and walked toward his office, beckoning his mate, who had heard the last part of the conversation, to go with him. They entered the office and the Captain locked the door, and taking a seat he exclaimed, " 'Pay well for the favor! 'I'll put him and his hound ashore as I promised, without reward, but as for those poor frightened fugitives, nothing was said about them, and there is not money enough in Kentucky to induce me to put them ashore with him. 'Pay well for the favor! 'I have already been paid well for the favor that shall be theirs."

Captain Titus was deeply affected, and sat some time apparently unable to speak. As soon as he could, he said to his mate, "William, you were not on that unfortunate boat with me when she was burned, and I think you never saw James B——, my colored steward on that boat. He was of the same race as the millions of men, women and children that are held in bondage under the flag that flies at our mast-head. The only shameful thing that can be said of the old flag is that it protects men in doing so foul a deed. I did not always feel so about it, in fact, I thought little about it one way or the other, but it is a live question with me now, and I will tell you how it came about, for I wish you to aid me in this matter, and hope to have your sympathy also. I will not recall the terrible scenes through which we passed in that awful hour. James stood by me to the last, and when the officers and crew had manned the boats and gone ashore with as many as they could carry, there were still men struggling in the water and trying to keep afloat until a vessel that was in sight could come to our rescue. James was a good swimmer, but I could not swim at all. The flames would soon drive us to the water, and I said, 'Could you swim ashore?' 'Oh, yes,' said he, 'easily enough, but Captain, I shall stay by you.' I felt sure there was no help for me, and that he could render me no assistance, so I urged him to try and save himself. He made no answer, and we were soon driven into the water; he gave me directions how to manage in holding on to him so as to leave him as free in his motions as possible. I cannot dwell on this subject. In short, I became too much exhausted to hold on to him, when he held me with one hand and sustained us both. I urged him to save himself, as I was sure he could not save both of us, but, said he, 'Captain, do you think I'll desert my best friend in such a place as this? No, sir! if you go down, we will go together.' When we were picked up I was insensible. I soon recovered, but he never entirely recovered. Now, William, you will have to wood up at Maiden, I suppose?" "Yes,—can't possibly go to Detroit without, you know."

When the boat approached the wharf at the old town of Maiden, Canada West, Curtis and Bill were playing cards. Looking up, they saw that the boat was stopping, and asked, "Where are we?" The answer was, "We are going to take on wood at Malden." "But this won't do," said Curtis, and he ran to find the Captain. To him he began to remonstrate in a violent manner, and Bill, meanwhile, was trying, by giving orders to the new hands, to prevent their landing; "but," said Curtis, "you agreed to land me in Michigan."

Capt.—"I'll do so when we get into the river."

Curtis.—"If you land here my niggers will escape."

Capt—"I can't help that, we can't go without wood."

Curtis.—"I'll give you a thousand dollars to land me and the niggers in Michigan."

Capt.—"I can't do it without wood."

Curtis.—"I shall hold you to your promise."

Capt.—"Of course you will; I'll land you, I did not promise to land your niggers."

Curtis now began to swear and use brutal language, when Captain Titus told him to stop that or he would have him arrested as soon as they should touch the wharf.

George and Clara were among the hands at the gangway, as they had been instructed by the mate, and when the plank was thrown out they ran into the town, Curtis and Bill after them, crying, "Stop, thief!" in great excitement. If they had taken time to think, they would not have ventured on shore; as it was, they were roughly handled, and glad when they found shelter on the boat again.

Some two years after, I was on a steamboat from Detroit to Cleveland; we stopped at Malden for wood, and while there I fell into conversation with an intelligent man, and inquired if he knew George and Clara, relating something of the above incidents. He said he knew them; they were prospering in business and much respected. He said that he saw the chase in the streets, and gave a very amusing account of the way the Kentucky gentlemen were handled.

CHAPTER IX.AN OLD-FASHIONED DEMOCRAT—THE U. G. R. R. BUSINESS A MEANS OF POLITICAL CONVERSION.

It often became necessary to obtain, on a sudden emergency, a considerable amount of funds in order to place large parties of fugitives beyond the power of the slave hunters. For that purpose certain individuals called on ladies and gentlemen, and stated the case without ever giving such information as could possibly betray the fugitives into any danger, and at such times men of all parties were solicited for aid. In pursuit of the aforesaid object, in the city of Albany, one of our solicitors called on an old gentleman who had long been, and was still, a leading man in the Democratic party. After hearing the statement, he said, "You want help to send these runaways to Canada, do you? I shall give nothing for any such purpose! Don't you see that it is against the law? Talk about human rights, human sympathies, self-evident principles, 'liberty and the pursuit of happiness;' such talk may have been very well once, but it is different now. Why, here is your Whig President, (Fillmore,) and that party, you know, claims to embody all the decency and all the religion in the nation—he would be down upon me with his fines and imprisonment, his marshals and his army. It is right to hold slaves, and wrong for them to run away. *Here are ten dollars to help pay their passage back;* give it to them, and advise them to go home and ask pardon for going off without leave, and if any more of them come along and need help to go home, don't fail to call on me—I like to help on a good cause."

That was many years ago, and many a ten-dollar bill did he give for the same object and with similar advice, still holding his standing good as a Democrat, until the Democratic party fired on the old flag at Sumter, since which time he has not been counted worthy of a name in the party; for copperheads are not made of such men as he—indeed, I do not know a man from whom we ever received aid and comfort in this enterprise, who is now in that party.

There are now living within twenty miles of Fredonia village, several men who were active agents on the U. G. R. R., and voted the Democratic ticket up to 1860, and others who had believed themselves Democrats "dyed in the wool," but had been converted from five to twenty years earlier just by the simple process of "taking stock" in this institution. I think I promised you some time ago that I would relate how a Democrat was converted in connection with the active business of the U. G. R. R., and as I once heard him relate the incident to a crowd of copperheads who had surrounded him in the town of Randolph, Cattaraugus Co., about the time that McClellan was nominated at Chicago, I will give it in his own language as near as I can recollect. The gentleman, Captain Chapman, I allude to, was a successful cultivator and dealer in fruits and garden vegetables, and being in Randolph one day with a load of fine fruit, his wagon was surrounded by a crowd of people of all classes, when a coppery old fellow remarked to the crowd that the fruit had a "niggery smell," and he didn't want any of it. Another man who had known him in his boyhood said, "Capt. C., you were brought up a Democrat of the straitest sect, and now you go for nigger equality, nigger voting, and marrying niggers, of course that will come next. I would like to know how a son of your father was ever turned over in this way."

"Well," said the Captain, "I can tell you how I was converted, though I don't understand how your talk about 'niggers,' as you call them, has anything to do with the flavor of my fruit, or with this question of maintaining our government when rebels are trying to destroy it; but seeing you want to know what's the matter with me, I'll tell you. It is true, as you say, my father was a Democrat, and perhaps he supposed that to hate a negro and to be a Democrat was all one thing,—can't say as to that, never heard him say much on the subject, though I remember a feeling of that sort seemed to be common. When I was a boy I wanted to go sailing on the lake, so father put me in care of Captain Perkins, and I became a sailor. By the time I was twenty-two years of age I was in command of a vessel on Lake Erie. We stopped at Cleveland one night, and the wind being high, we anchored in the harbor, but about daybreak the wind fell away and we started for Buffalo. When about three miles out, a boat with four men in it put off from the shore and came towards us with a white flag flying, so we hove to until the boat came alongside. Two of the men were merchants in Cleveland, with whom I was well acquainted—had done business with them the day before; one of them threw on board a purse, containing about $15 in silver, and said, 'Land these two men in Canada, take your pay out of that and give them what is left.' The two men came aboard and the boat returned.

"The men thrown upon my hands were very black, coarse in feature and build, stupid in expression, and apparently incapable of any mental excitement except fear. They were frightened out of their wits if they ever had any, and started involuntarily at every noise, but sat upon the deck and soon fell asleep. An hour or two after I saw a steamer coming out of Cleveland harbor, and when she had passed nearly a mile away, she turned and came toward us. I took my glass and looked at her, and saw a man with a glass scanning my vessel. After coming near enough to see distinctly all that was on my deck, they bore away on their course to Buffalo. I knew, of course, that these men were fugitive slaves, though they were the first that I had ever seen. I had heard it remarked that it was only the smartest niggers that ever got away, and thought I, if these are the smartest, what stupid animals the masses of the slaves must be; although I have since seen many of them escaping by the U. G. R. R., I still think these appeared the most stupid and degraded specimens I have ever seen. They would not talk, and seemed incapable of giving an intelligible account of their escape, or from whence they came, except that they had lived somewhere in Virginia on a tobacco plantation, were sold and driven with a large coffle in chains to the Ohio River, and shipped for 'down river.' They left the boat and got ashore, were taken in charge by the agents of the U. G. R. R., though at the time I had never heard of that institution, and my vessel was pressed into the service, and constituted an 'extension of the track' without my knowing it; as to their progress after they landed in Ohio, I learned that afterwards. While they were on my vessel I felt little interest in them, and had no idea that the love of liberty as a part of man's nature was in the least possible degree felt or understood by them. Before entering Buffalo harbor, I ran in near the Canada shore, manned a boat and landed them on the beach. I then handed to them the purse and all its contents, and told them that they were free. They said, 'Is this Canada?' I said, 'Yes, there are no slaves in this country;' then I witnessed a scene I shall never forget. They seemed to be transformed; a new light shone in their eyes, their tongues were loosed, they laughed and cried, prayed and sang praises, fell upon the ground and kissed it over and over, embraced a tree and kissed it, hugged and kissed each other, crying, 'Bress de Lord! Oh! I'se free before I die!'

"I wish," said the Captain, "you could all have seen it; there is no use trying to describe it, I can't do justice to the subject. I left them and returned to my vessel, and while returning I thought to myself, 'My God! is it possible that human beings are kept in such a condition that they are made perfectly happy by being landed and left alone in a strange land with no human beings or habitation in sight, with the prospect of never seeing a friend or relative, without a single bright spot or prospect in the future, except the single idea—Liberty? And who is to blame?' Before I stepped upon my deck I had determined to never again be identified with any party that sustained the system of slavery, and, gentlemen, it is my opinion that there is not a copperhead rebel in this crowd who is as capable of appreciating the true principles of human liberty, and of enjoying the practical application of such principles as were those poor stupid slaves. Why, just look at the facts. The former masters of those slaves are your masters. They call you 'mudsills,' subsisting by labor; the best of you, if known to live by your own labor, even if it were only selling goods or teaching school, would not be allowed to sit at their tables, and if you travel into their territory you must padlock your jaws. And what is the result? Have you accepted emancipation when offered? for in the emancipation of the negro your own is secured. Do you accept it and rejoice in it? Not a bit of it; you would reject it if it were not forced upon you. While you sneer at and slander the negro for accepting his freedom, you go down in the dirt and lick the heels of the men who trample on you, and tell you that labor degrades you, and then straighten yourselves up and judge of the right of a class of men to vote by the color of their skin, as if that were the only thing in which your claim to the right of suffrage would bear competition with theirs." The Captain had been interrupted two or three times, and a large crowd had gathered around him. He was about offering his fruit for sale again, when some one asked, "How about the man on the steamboat?" "Well," said he, "before I was fairly fastened to the wharf two men came on board and asked to be shown 'where I had put those colored men?' 'What colored men?' I replied. 'The niggers,' said one, 'that you brought from Cleveland.' 'There were no such men on this vessel when I left Cleveland,' I replied. 'I saw them,' he said, 'from the steamer when we passed you, and I shall search the vessel.' 'Well,' I said, 'search it if you want to, you will find no such men on this craft.' "However, I thought, as a little excitement would be rather pleasant just then, I would tell him all about it, withholding the account of how they came on board, and I did tell him, not forgetting their conduct when they found they were free. The man turned pale, trembled, grated his teeth, walked up and down the deck, and finally having recovered his voice,—he was so mad at first he could not speak—he shook his fist at me, keeping, however, at safe distance, and said, with horrid oaths, 'You shall suffer for this!' I said, 'Sir, it is not proper to speak in that manner to a Captain on his own ship.' He appeared to understand me, and left the vessel. I never heard from him again"

CHAPTER X.TWO DEMOCRATIC NEIGHBORS VOTE FOR JAMES K. POLK AND HAVE A VISIT THE EVENING AFTER ELECTION— THEY BECOME U. G. R. R. AGENTS—THE ESCAPE OF ROBERT.

While waiting for a train at Perrysburgh, Cattaraugus Co., a few days ago, I met my old friend, Wm, Cooper, Esq. When I first knew him, Mr. Cooper was Supervisor of that town, and he was several times re-elected by the Democratic party; indeed, he was the most influential Democrat in that part of the county, until in an unguarded hour he became interested in the U. G, R. R. He said, the other day, that he was terribly convicted the first time he heard a fugitive relate his sufferings in slavery, and his adventures in making his escape. The wickedness and the danger of sustaining such a system, and the hypocrisy of the political parties, each of which strained every nerve to convince the South that the other was opposed to slavery, convinced him that there was no choice between them on that question; but at the next election he voted, as usual, the "Loco Foco" ticket. The election had been held at his house, (he kept a hotel,) and after the votes had been counted and the people had all gone home except a neighbor and fellow Democrat, he said, "Patch, I have voted for a slaveholder for President for the last time;" and Patch answered, "So have I, but then what are we to do? The Whigs are as careful to have a slaveholder on their ticket as our party." "True," said Cooper, "but this new party, the Birney Party, that polled but three votes in this town to-day, is destined to be successful. It may not succeed as a party, but the principles of the Declaration of Independence, as embodied in their platform will succeed. The people of this nation will not always he fooled by party demagogues, and one or the other of the leading parties will eventually adopt the radical principles of the men who fought England to secure liberty for all the people. We may have to fight again, but, sir, I tell you that whatever party leaders and unprincipled politicians may do, the people will stand by the right, and when aroused to a sense of the condition to which we are drifting, parties and politicians must stand aside. Leading men in the South have an idea that the North will submit to anything for peace, and acting upon that idea, they are in the habit of carrying all their points by threatening to dissolve the Union and boasting of their fighting qualities, but they will learn that this universal Yankee nation, much as we like peace and money making, if a dirty, disagreeable job must be done, will astonish the world by our manner of doing it." "Well," said Patch, "I was not aware that you had surrendered to these radicals. I had made up my mind to help whip the Whigs, for by so doing I should vote against a slaveholder as well as for one, which I flatter myself would balance that account. I have noticed that in attacking this little party, finding nothing in their principles to which they can safely object, both the Whigs and Democrats charge them with radicalism. Radicalism, as I understand it, is a determination to do right because it is right, and refusing to do wrong because it is wrong, while the Whigs and Democrats, by their own platforms, show that the conservatism by which they propose to demolish each other, is merely going halves with the devil."

That year business on the U. G. Road became very active, and both the above gentlemen became zealous agents. They had seen some service before, and that explained in some measure "what was the matter." The first arrival at our station, direct from that of Captain Cooper, came in charge of his son as conductor. The name of the fugitive, or the name by which he called himself, was Robert. He was evidently a very valuable man, and had escaped from a party of Congressmen on their way to Washington from Mississippi, one of whom was his master, and as he said, his half brother. He escaped from some point between Wheeling and Baltimore, and made his journey across Pennsylvania in a rambling way, suffering incredible hardships, hunger, and almost nakedness. His home had been so far from the Free States that he had never heard of this institution, therefore he dared not apply for aid. When almost starved, he fell into the hands of one of our agents south of Jamestown, near the State line, thence came through Ellington, Leon, Dayton and Perrysburgh, arriving at our station early in the evening.

He had been so long wandering in the Pennsylvania mountains that we supposed the pursuit must, of course, have been abandoned, and this idea nearly proved fatal. The spies along the lake shore came near eluding the vigilance of our agents, and had established a strict watch at new points, but they were trapped by the proslavery conversation of one of our detectives, and the fact was disclosed that there was "danger." So close were the slave-hunters upon Robert's track that he was obliged to turn backward, and passed our place in the evening. The hunter, coming from the east, crossed the river into the village just about the time that Robert disappeared south into the woods. One of our best guides was with him, and before the next morning delivered him to Mr. Welles, in Leon. A few days after he was placed in the hands of a Quaker friend, named Hathaway, in Collins, Erie Co. In the meantime the hunter was spying around Forestville. The Quaker friend had a house in the woods, where during the season he made maple sugar, and there Robert stayed until the hunters withdrew, when he went to Madison Co. He tried hard to learn to read and write, and succeeded partially, though he made slow progress. He used to say that when slavery was abolished, he would go back to Mississippi and preach to the colored people, and often expressed a wish to go to school and prepare himself for mission work. He came back to Chautauqua Co. a year or two before the war, and worked at chopping wood one winter. He had heard nothing from his old home in many years, yet his faith was unshaken that he should go back a free man, and preach to the colored people there in the far south. When I last saw him, he spoke of going to the negro settlement in Canada as soon as he could finish his job, since which I have not heard from him.

The few incidents related in these sketches, much from memory, aided by very limited search among memoranda, read so tamely compared with the interest and excitement that was felt at the time, that they seem hardly worth relating yet the liberation. of a single human being from so wicked and loathsome a degradation as that of American slavery, is worth more than all the sacrifice it ever cost. But it should not be supposed that the rescue of here and there an individual from bondage was the sole object proposed to be accomplished by the establishment of the U. G. R. R., and I think that when its history shall be understood, it will be known that it did more to hasten the crisis and final clash of arms that resulted in making this a free nation than any other agency. But for this, the fugitive slave law would not have been enacted, and but for that law, we should still have been under the heel of the slave oligarchy. Besides, in its silent operations it is wonderful how much humanity was sifted out of the old Democratic organization, leaving only Copperhead treason trying to shelter itself under the name of that old party.

CHAPTER XI.TRUE DEMOCRATS VERSUS COPPERHEADS—THE ESCAPE OF STATIE AND LILA—FROM WASHINGTON, D. C., TO WARSAW, N. Y., IN A BOX—PURSUERS FOILED.

When Owen Lovejoy made his great speech on the bill to repeal the "black laws" of the State of Illinois, he denounced the fugitive slave law as not only wicked and unjust, unnatural and dangerous to the stability of a free government, but also mean and degrading, an outrage on every principle of humanity and religion. He endorsed the U. G. R. R. in all its principles, actions and results, and closed his speech by saying, "In so doing I accept the consequences of wicked legislation, and let it be known that Owen Lovejoy, of Princeton, Bureau Co., Illinois, will hold himself ready at all times to give advice, food, shelter and aid in every possible way, in the pursuit of freedom, to any poor, panting fugitive from the horrors of American slavery, so help me Almighty God."

It had been announced that Lovejoy was to speak on the bill, and the State House at Springfield was crowded with ladies and gentlemen of all parties. When going home, a leading Democrat, holding one of the highest offices in the State, was leading by the hand his little daughter, his particular favorite, whom he had taken with him to hear Mr. Lovejoy's speech. Having walked some distance without speaking, she said, "Is that man an abolitionist?" "Yes," said he. "Well, papa, are you an abolitionist too?" "Yes," he replied, "but I was such a d——d (feeling the pressure of the soft little hand, he felt admonished to skip the hard words, and hesitating a little, said), "I was such a fool that I didn't know it!" The above incident was related to me by a man who was a member of the Legislature, was present and heard the speech, and was acquainted with all the parties, and it is mentioned here to show that men were sometimes Democrats who had none of the *copperhead* virus in them. Of this class was one of the principal actors in the sketch which follows:

I was stopping over night in the village of Attica, Wyoming Co., N. Y., and while transacting business in the town I chanced to meet Col. Charles O. Shepard, a very popular member of the State Senate, an active member of the liberty party, and one of the original stockholders in this institution. Mr. Shepard invited me to take breakfast with him, saying that he had something he would like to show me. I accepted the invitation, and after breakfast he showed me an U. G. R. R. car, in which two fugitives had come all the way from Washington, D. C. It was a box, made of light boards, to fit into a gardener's market wagon; the forepart formed a seat, and the back part was high, so that a person could sit on the bottom, extending the feet forward under the driver's seat. In this box a woman and her daughter had, a few days before, arrived at his house from Washington without change of horses or driver.

Some 22 years since, several farmers in Onondaga Co., having some money to invest, went to the District of Columbia and to counties in Virginia near Washington, and bought old, worn out farms at from $5 to $15 per acre, and by the use of fertilizers and the application of their northern system of farming, they brought them into profitable cultivation. Three or four of these men were my school-mates when we were boys. They bought no slaves, but hired them of their masters to aid in cultivating the land, etc. A man by the name of Lines lived just over the line in Virginia, who owned more slaves than he could employ, therefore he hired them out, and the wages he received for their labor constituted his income, selling one occasionally to supply any deficiency. One of the women whom he thus robbed of the wages she earned, was a remarkably efficient house servant, by the name of Statie. Her master allowed her to hire herself out on condition that she paid him $10 per month, and also furnished clothing for her little daughter, Lila, at that time about seven years of age. The mother and daughter were both nearly white. Statie hired herself for a year to one of the above named northern farmers, whose principal business was market gardening, and while she lived in the family as house servant, she was allowed the privilege of keeping her little girl with her for several weeks at a time. The little girl was of a sunny temper, very pretty, and both active and intelligent for one of her age, and the family of Mr. Barbour, with whom they lived, became attached to both the child and her mother.

At the end of the year a hotel keeper in Washington, having heard of the superior qualification of Statie as a cook, offered her more wages, and as she was trying to lay by money to buy the freedom of her child, she went to live in Washington, and her child stayed on the plantation, some 10 miles offin Virginia. Statie was allowed to go home once in three months to see her child and pay her wages to her master. On one of these occasions she learned that a slave trader had been trying to buy Lila, and her master had gone so far as to set a time when he would answer as to terms of sale. Statie, though in great distress, had sufficient presence of mind to conceal her feelings, and talked cheerfully to L. when she paid him her quarter's wages, about the time when she hoped to be able to buy Lila's freedom, a subject that she seldom failed to allude to when paying money to her master. As it was two or three months before the trader would be there, and possibly realizing something of the cruelty he proposed inflicting on both mother and daughter, and softened by the receipt of her quarter's wages and her cheerful talk, he consented to let Lila go with her mother for a few weeks. Remembering the kindness of Mr. Barbour's family, she walked many miles out of her way in returning to Washington to lay her troubles before them. Barbour and his wife were shocked at the idea of their little favorite being sold away from her mother, and a plan was soon arranged, whereby Mr. Barbour met Statie late in the evening of the following Wednesday on a country road a mile or two outside of the city. Statie and her child were fixed comfortably in the aforesaid box, which had been supplied with straw, and as many conveniences as could be arranged. Barbour managed to get into Pennsylvania as soon as possible, but fearing pursuers, he kept them out of sight until they arrived in Wyoming Co., N. Y.

When out of sight of settlements, they sometimes went out and picked berries, and when safe to do so they walked about in the night. He stopped at taverns or farm houses, leaving the wagon in the barn. The wagon was what is called in that country a "Jersey wagon," having six posts and covered with oil cloth. When inquired of as to the contents of the box he said he had been peddling clocks, and was going home to York State, and as he drove a splendid team his word was taken without examination.

Knowing Col. S., not personally, but by reputation, as a safe agent of the U. G. R. R., he thought it best to take the fugitives to him; therefore he came through the mountain district of Pa., striking the State line near Wellsville, in Alleghany Co., went direct to Warsaw, and put up at a hotel, where he inquired if the landlord knew such a man as Col. C. O. Shepard. "Yes," said the landlord, "and he is here attending court." Statie and Lila were then brought into the house and were warmly greeted by the crowd of people, it being the first time they had been seen, except by Mr. Barbour, since they left Washington. Col. S. took charge of them and asked the privilege of keeping the box in which they came as a relic, and Mr. Barbour went to his old home in Onondaga Co. No suspicion ever rested on Mr. Barbour in Virginia as to his agency in the escape of the fugitives. He had talked of going north about that time, and then his political opinions were a sufficient guaranty. What he had seen of slavery had little effect upon his feelings and opinions, and he was regarded as pro-slavery as were all Democrats everywhere, but he took an interest in the fate of this poor child and her almost distracted mother, and determined to save them at all hazards. A few days' active service on the U. G. R. R. proved too much for his prejudices, and *his vote never went in that direction again.*

A few days after Col. S. came home, bringing the fugitives with him from Warsaw, two strangers rode up in front of the Post Office in the village of Attica, and inquired if the Postmaster was within, judging, of course, that the Postmaster must be sound on the slave question. There were disappointed in not finding that official ready to aid them in reclaiming a fugitive.

They were in pursuit of Statie and her child. An account of their arrival in Wyoming Co. had got into the local papers, by which means Lines had learned where they might probably be found, and employed these men to capture them. The Postmaster took them into his office and told them plainly that the slaves were within half a mile of the village, "but," said he, "you had better not try to take them. I would be glad to help you if I dared to, but every man, woman and child in the place would help them, and you can't raise men enough in this county to take them away from here. I see by the commotion in the streets that you are suspected already, and I cannot answer for your safety if you should ever attempt to prosecute this business. Such a thing has never been attempted here, and I tell you it will go hard with the man that tries it. Now," said he, "I have nothing more to say on the subject, except that I should think fifteen or twenty minutes is as long a time as it will be safe for you to be seen in this town. A glance at the crowd already gathered in the street was sufficient to clinch the arguments of the Postmaster, so the slave hunters mounted their horses and rode silently out of town, the people making no demonstration until they were on the bridge, when a shout, a cheer, three times three, seemed to put new life into their horses, and they were soon out of sight. In the office they threatened to return with force sufficient to execute their purpose, but they never came, though Col. S. thought best to send the fugitives into another part of the county, and their retreat was for a long time kept secret.

A gentleman who lives in Attica told me a few days ago that Lila still lives in Wyoming Co., a respectable, intelligent woman, but her mother died within two years after she came there.

CHAPTER XII.MARGARET BORN ON A SLAVE SHIP—CHILDHOOD IN A KIND FAMILY—ANOTHER MASTER, WICKED, CRUEL, AND A COWARD—HER HUSBAND SOLD AND SHE ESCAPES—HUNTED WITH BLOOD-HOUNDS AND RESCUED BY A MASTIFF—ARRIVES IN NEW YORK—HER SON, SAMUEL R. WARD.

On the eastern shore of the Chesapeake, in the State of Maryland, there lived, about forty years ago, a remarkable woman by the name of Margaret. She was born on a slave ship on its way from Africa to Baltimore, just before the importation of slaves was prohibited. She, with her mother, fell into the hands of a family who gave them religious instruction, and Margaret, while young, exhibited traits of character that were regarded as remarkable for one of her race. Of a proud, indomitable spirit, yet having acute moral sense, a disposition naturally amiable, of cheerful temperament, and crushed with a sense of her degraded condition, she was unusually capable in all kinds of housework, and especially active and competent as nurse when any of the family were sick. By observation she learned the polite manners and graceful deportment of ladies of the family and those who visited there. Her obedience to every command, her kindness to any one who was in trouble, and polite deportment toward all, seemed to be the result of a conscientious desire to imitate her Saviour whom she had early learned to love.

At sixteen years of age she went to live with her young mistress, who was married to a planter in that fertile country known as the "Eastern Shore." At eighteen Margaret was a large woman, tall and well formed, her complexion black as jet, her countenance always pleasant, though she seldom laughed. She talked but little, even to those of her own race. At twenty years of age she became the wife of a worthy young man to whom she had given her best affections. Not long after, her young master became very angry with her for what he called stubbornness and resistance to his will, and threatened to chastise her by whipping—a degradation that she had always felt that she could not submit to, and yet to obey her master in the thing he demanded would be still worse. She therefore told him that she would not be whipped, she would rather die, and gave him warning that any attempt to execute his threat would surely result in the death of one of them. He knew her too well to risk the experiment, and decided to punish her in another way. He sold her husband, and she saw him bound in chains and driven off with a large drove of men and women for the New Orleans market. He then put her in the hands of a brutal overseer, with directions to work her to the extent of her ability on a tobacco plantation, which command was enforced up to the day of the birth of her child. At the end of one week she was driven again to the field and compelled to perform a full task, having at no time any abatement of her work on account of her situation, with the exception of one week. It was the custom on the plantations to establish nurseries, presided over by old, broken down slaves, where mothers might leave their infants during the work hours, but this privilege was denied to Margaret. She was obliged to leave her child under the shade of a bush in the field, returning to it but twice during the long day. On returning to the child one evening she found it apparently senseless, exhausted with crying, and a large serpent lying across it. Although she felt that it would be better for both herself and child if it were dead, yet a mother's heart impelled her to make an effort to save it, and by caressing and careful handling she resuscitated it. As soon as she heard its feeble, wailing cry, she made a vow to deliver her boy from the cruel power of slavery or die in the attempt, and falling prostrate, she prayed for strength to perform her vow, and for grace and patience to sustain her in her suffering, toil and hunger; then pressing her child to her bosom, she fled with all the speed of which she was capable toward the North Star. Having gone a mile or two, she heard something pursuing her; on looking round she saw Watch, the old house dog. Watch was a large mastiff, somewhat old, and with him Margaret had ever been a favorite, and since she had been driven to the field, Watch often visited her at her cabin in the evening. She feared it would not be safe to allow Watch to go with her, but she could not induce him to go back, so she resumed her flight, accompanied by her faithful escort. At break of day she hid herself on the border of a plantation and soon fell asleep.

Toward evening she was aroused by the noise made by the slaves returning to their quarters, and seeing an old woman lingering behind all the others, she called her, told her troubles and asked for food. The old woman returned about midnight with a pretty good supply of food, which Margaret divided with Watch, and then started on taking the north star for her guide. The second day after she left, the Overseer employed a hunter with his dogs to find her. He started with an old slut and three whelps, thinking, no doubt, that as the game was only a woman and her infant child, it would be a good time to train his pups. Margaret had been missed at roll call the morning after her flight, but the Overseer supposed she was hiding near the place for a day or two, and that hunger would soon drive her up; therefore, when the hunter started, he led the old dog, expecting to find her in an hour or two, but not overtaking her the first day, on the next morning he let his hounds loose, intending to follow on horseback, guided by their voices. About noon, the old dog struck the track at the place where Margaret had made her little camp the day before, and she bounded off with fresh vigor, leaving the man and the younger dogs beyond sight and hearing. The young dogs soon lost the track where Margaret forded the streams, and the old dog was miles away, leaving the hunter without a guide to direct him.

Margaret had been lying in the woods on the bank of a river, intending to start again as soon as it was dark, when she was startled by the whining and nervous motions of old Watch, and listening, she heard the hoarse ringing bay of a blood-hound. Although she had expected that she would be hunted with dogs, and recalled over and over again the shocking accounts related by Overseers to the slaves, of fugitives overtaken and torn in pieces by the savage Spanish blood-hounds, she had not, until now, realized the horrors of her situation. She expected to have to witness the destruction of her child by the savage brute, and then be torn in pieces herself She did not, however, lose her presence of mind. The river or inlet near her camp was too wide and too deep to be forded at that place, but she fastened her child to her shoulders and waded in as far as she could, taking a club to defend herself. Meanwhile, old Watch lay with his nose between his feet, facing the coming foe. The hound, rendered more fierce by the freshness of the track, came rushing headlong with nose to the ground, scenting her prey, and seemed not to see old Watch, until, leaping to pass over him, she found her wind-pipe suddenly collapsed in the massive jaws of the old mastiff. The struggle was not very noisy, for Watch would not even growl, and the hound could not, but it was terribly energetic. The hound made rapid and persuasive gestures with her paws and tail, but it was of no use, the jaws of old Watch relaxed not until all signs of life in his enemy had ceased. Margaret came back from the river, and would have embraced her faithful friend, but fearing that a stronger pack was following, she hastily threw the dead hound into the river and pursued her journey.

It would make this sketch too long to relate all Margaret's adventures before she reached New York City, where she lived many years. Within a few hours after her providential escape by the aid of her faithful friend, old Watch, from the fangs of the slave hunter's hound, she fell into the hands of friends, who kept her secreted until she could be sent into a free State; while there, she learned about the pursuit by the hunter, and that he never knew what became of his best hound. After the chase was abandoned, she, through a regular line, similar to our U. G. R. R., was sent to Philadelphia and then to New York, where she became a celebrated nurse, and always befriended the poor of all colors and all nationalities. She rented a good house which was a home for herself and boy, and also for old Watch while he lived. When her boy, whom she called Samuel, was old enough to go to school, she found a place for him in Westchester Co., where he obtained the rudiments of an education, and afterwards in the family of a gentleman in Central New York, he enjoyed the advantages of a thorough education, and became a devoted minister of the gospel in the Congregational Church. I often met him during the early history of the U. G. R. R., of which he was an efficient agent. Samuel was one of the most eloquent men I have ever heard speak. He was a fine looking man, though he was so black it was sometimes said that it grew dark when he entered a room; but it grew light when he began to speak. I never saw Margaret, but I have heard Samuel relate her sufferings and adventures, and describe her loving kindness to him and her self-sacrificing devotion to the interests of suffering humanity, in language and expression such as I never dare try to imitate. He was well informed, and knew the history of our country better than some men who make greater pretensions, in illustration of which I will relate, as well as I can, an incident at which several ladies and gentlemen who witnessed it were much amused.

It was at a time when a stirring political campaign excited all classes. In a parlor at a hotel a man was giving his opinions on political affairs in a voice loud enough for all in the room to hear. His theme was the abuse that the North had heaped upon the South. The man had been introduced to gentlemen in the room as the Rev. Mr. , though one person told me that all the use he had made of his claim to the sacred office for thirty years had been to demand exemption from taxes on the ground of being a clergyman. He proceeded to eulogize the Southerners as a brave, noble, refined people, suffering untold abuse and calumny from the whole North except his party; it was a state of things not to be put up with much longer; the slaveholders and their Democratic friends were going to settle the question with the bayonet! "Well," said a gentleman from Vermont, to whom the discourse seemed to be directed, "please tell us wherein we have abused our friends down South." "I'll tell you," said he, "here's this State of New York; finding the climate and other things unfavorable to slavery, they passed a law abolishing it, to take effect in twenty years, for the purpose of giving time to run off all the slaves and sell them, so that when the time arrived, the slaves had all been sold, and now we are demanding the liberation of the slaves for which we have pocketed the money." Samuel had stopped there for the night and sat by the table apparently reading, while he listened to the conversation. As the Vermonter made no answer, Samuel turned his face towards the reverend gentleman and said, "Are you not mistaken in relation to this matter?" The reverend looked at him scornfully, as if he would decline talking with a black man, but as he liked to dispute better than he liked anything else except money and aristocracy, and no doubt expecting to wipe out the black spot, he said, "What do you know about it?" "I know," replied Sam, "that not a slave was ever legally sold to be taken out of this State, or taken out of the State to be sold, after the passage of the law abolishing slavery. The law itself made it a penal offense to do so, and even a Congressman could not take his slave servant to Washington without giving bonds of $1,000 to return him to this State. No, sir, the slaves were not sold out of the State!" The statement was made in such a prompt, downright manner, that Rev.—— dared not dispute it, but went on to say that "Massachusetts was less particular in her legislation. After realizing cash for every slave owned in the State, they are arrogantly demanding freedom for the same and all the rest of the slaves, and making more disturbance than all the other States put together."

"Begging your pardon," said Sam, "I wish to say that you were pointed out to me as the man who owns the best library in this County. Most surely, sir, you have read history to little purpose if you do not know that slavery was not abolished in Massachusetts by legislation, and that not an hour was allowed those who held slaves in that State in which they might sell or run them off." "This is a precious piece of nonsense you are relating," said, "who does not know that Massachusetts was once a slave State, and that it is now one of the free States?" "True," said Samuel, "but there was no gradual emancipation nor selling of slaves, and there was no legislation about it. When Massachusetts became a State, and the people of the State adopted a constitution, the preamble, or, as they called it, their bill of rights, was copied almost verbatim from the preamble of the Declaration of Independence, which declares, briefly, that all men have equal rights, and have equal right to protection in the enjoyment thereof. As soon as the constitution was adopted by the people, a gentleman residing in Hampden Co., who could not have been a Democrat of your stamp, though he held nine or ten slaves, said to his foreman, a very intelligent slave, "Thomas, I think you are legally entitled to freedom. I have thought about it a long time, especially since we have declared our independence, and are sacrificing thousands of lives and millions of property in defense of the principles that we publish to the world as our excuse for so doing; and now our State having embodied the same principle into the constitution as the fundamental law of the State, you are as much entitled to freedom as I am. To test this question, I wish you to employ counsel and bring a suit against me in the Supreme Court for illegally holding you in slavery, urging your claim under the bill of rights in the constitution. You will need money to retain a lawyer, and here are a hundred dollars which you can use for that purpose." I need not relate the proceedings in detail—if you desire to know the history of emancipation in Massachusetts, you can, no doubt, find it in your library. I will only say, to substantiate my first statement, that the suit was commenced and carried through to the highest court, and decided every time in favor of Thomas, his master paying all costs and counsel fees. When it had been decided in the last court, the Governor of the State made proclamation that all persons heretofore held as slaves in Massachusetts were free, and warned all persons against buying or selling, or in any way treating them as slaves, and guaranteed to them all the rights of citizens of the State, since which time people in that State transact all kinds of business without question as to the color of their skin. For the rest, as to how the people north and south treat each other, and the position they occupy before the world in regard to education, refinement, enterprise and Christian civilization, I respectfully refer you to the debate between Webster and Hayne, which, of course, may be found in your library."

I have met —— but once since, and that was in 1863, when he was holding forth to a crowd on the beauties of the southern system of labor, southern refinement, etc., and predicting that after they had thrashed us at the North, there would be some hope of our improvement. The last I heard of Samuel he went to England, and was sent by the government on a mission of some kind to Jamaica, W. I.

CHAPTER XIII.THE ESCAPE OF JIM AND HIS COMPANIONS— NIGHT MEETINGS AMONG THE SLAVES—AN ANGRY SOUTHERNER IN FREDONIA.

Three fugitives arrived at our station about 8 o'clock one night in January, 18—. They came in a sleigh, covered with robes and blankets so that no person was to be seen. The load had the appearance of a load of grain protected from the snow on a stormy day. They had been pushed forward from Painesville, Ohio, in a very secret way, changing conductors every day, or at midnight, as was the case sometimes; the conductor who brought them to our place had started in the afternoon, and had driven twenty miles through the drifting snow. As the night was dark and the road toward Black Rock not well beaten, we thought we might venture to wait until five o'clock in the morning before we sent them forward. They had been obliged to deviate from the most direct line two or three times, being closely chased by an experienced hunter who had "bought them running," or at his own risk. Our detectives had misled the fellow, and although we hoped he had become discouraged and gone home, we determined to be careful, and it was well we did.

Rev. Mr. Frink was in our village that evening on a visit to his brother who lived there. Mr. Frink kept a station on the U. G. R. R., in Chautauqua Co., therefore I invited him to have a talk with the fugitives, and also to give us the benefit of his counsel about getting them through. One of the boys, named Jim, gave us an interesting account of their adventures. He was a shrewd fellow, and had not intended to run away until the day they started, when he decided to come for the sake of the other two, for, said he, "They couldn't come without me, they didn't know how." They were his particular friends; he thought a "heap" of them, and their mother had learned that they were to be sent South in a drove soon after Christmas. The two boys had always been kept on the plantation, had seldom been beyond its boundaries, while he (Jim) had been a kind of sub-over, seer, had been sent to market to assist in driving mules, sometimes had charge of a gang of hands, and was therefore more competent to "find the way out" than the other boys were, and was finally persuaded by their old mother to go with them.

They had been provided with passes to spend Christmas with their relatives on another plantation, but hoping to find friends in another direction, they started towards the Ohio River, sixty miles off. The Christmas festivities, which were being celebrated by the slaves on all the plantations, enabled them to supply themselves with food and shelter at the slave quarters along the way. The weather was unusually cold, and they expected trouble in. crossing the Ohio, but when they arrived at the river, above Parkersburg, in Virginia, they found it frozen over—very unconstitutional behavior, certainly, on the part of the river, but as their education had been neglected, it could not be expected that the poor fellows would know that it would be wrong for them to avail themselves of the illegal acts of the Ohio River, so they crossed over on the ice. Never having heard of the U. G. R. R., they had skulked and stumbled along half the way to Lake Erie before they fell into the hands of our agents.

The first hint that our folks received in relation to them came from the hunters who followed them. They had crossed over into Ohio and begun inquiring for them, when one fell into the company of one of our detectives, who, pretending to sympathize with the scamp, agreed to do what he could to find the track, though I am not sure that he promised to show it to him when he found it. It was soon known in all directions by our agents and conductors that there was "game abroad and hunters close upon the track," and as they knew the run-ways better than the hunters from Virginia, they soon had the boys under their protection.

Judge Paine in northern Ohio, one of our most enterprising Superintendents, directed their movements, and it required all his tact and energy to run them through.

When they had related their adventures and hairbreadth escapes, Rev. Mr. Frink said, "Jim, you told us that you had not intended to come away till you were persuaded to help the boys; now I want to know the reason why you preferred slavery to freedom, when these boys, who evidently do not know half as much as you do, were willing to risk their, lives to obtain liberty." "That's it," said Jim, "that's the very thing. They don't know. Some don't know and some does. Niggers that know isn't all alike; there is two sorts; some is afraid and they run off as soon as they can, others are not afraid and they will stick by their people." "You say," said Mr. Frink, "that some know and some don't know. What do you mean by that?" "Well," said Jim, "it may be you have heard of Nat Turner and his insurrection." "Yes," said Mr. Frink. "Well," said Jim, "some of the slaves know all about that, and they talk about it all over Virginia, and Kentucky, and Car'lina, and everywhere. They have meetings in the night; they go this way and that way, and tell what is going on everywhere; so you see we agree which way is best. We think Nat Turner was a good man, but he couldn't do much to make us all free, though he scared the white folks awfully. Then they hung Nat Turner, and them that know, say it is best not to try that way again. We hear that a great many white folks are trying to make us all free, and our masters say they will have war and whip the Yankees, and some of us agree to stay and maybe we can do something to help." "How did you hear all this?" said Frink. "Well," said Jim," when they make a President, and the Democrats have a barbecue, and make great speeches and talk big, they say the *Whigs* are going to free all our niggers, and the Whigs have a barbecue and talk big, and say the *Democrats* are going to free all the niggers, and more than that, they are going to *burn their barns*. Now, you see, when old master goes to barbecue, he takes servants along to see to the horses and take care of the old man when he gets drunk, and of course they hear it all, and when we have a meeting they tell all about it. We can't understand what it all means, but one thing is sure, they get madder and madder every time, and when they come to blows, I always intended to help the side that would help us, whichever that was."

As Jim appeared to understand about those "meetings in the night" better than any other we had met, we talked with him until we learned where and through whom we could communicate with the knowing ones, and not long after we were able to make connections and open lines far down in the slave States. The leaders of the meetings in the night, meanwhile, were being educated as to who their friends were, and the first gun on Sumter was the signal for an entire change in the operations of the U. G. R. R., *and those who had been helped became the helpers*. The experienced agents and conductors, black though they were, piloted many a white soldier, escaped from Andersonville, Belle Isle, and Libby prison, through swamps and mountain passes to the Union lines, thus repaying all the time and treasure that had been expended in their behalf by this institution. Indeed, for this service, this branch of the U. G. R. R., with negro conductors, was more efficient than any red tape or military organization could have been made, as multitudes of escaped prisoners gratefully testify.

A few weeks after this I was reminded of what Jim said about those meetings in the night, by reading in one of our popular magazines an incident related by a slaveholder to a gentleman who was visiting at his plantation in the sea island cotton region. The slaveholder, whose name was Poindexter, said to his friend, Mr. Hill, "I am exceedingly perplexed about what course to pursue in relation to my negroes. I was surprised, and not a little amused, by what I saw last night. My boy Tom oversees all my hands on this plantation, is the best manager in the county, makes the best crops with the least trouble; he never whips, and there is no skulking and no sham sickness. He is a Baptist preacher, and all the slaves for miles around come every Sunday to hear him preach. There is, as Tom says, 'a powerful revival' in these parts, and he has many times during the past month asked for a pass to go to an island near at hand to hold a meeting in the night, and as he is always on hand in the morning, I usually let him go. Having noticed an unusual sadness in Tom's countenance of late, and other things in his deportment that seemed peculiar, my curiosity was excited, and I concluded to follow him last night to witness his manner of holding his meeting. He crossed the narrow inlet to the island on the trunk of a fallen tree, and instead of going towards the plantation he struck into a narrow path leading through thick bushes towards a dense forest. I managed to follow him nearly half a mile into the woods, when I saw the light of a large fire shining on the tall trees. A few men were sitting around on logs, and others constantly coming, but no women or children. I hid myself near the cleared spot and waited until almost midnight, when I saw a man approach the fire towards whom the negroes (as many as a hundred had arrived), showed a marked respect. He immediately stepped on to a stump and commenced a speech, having first called on Tom to say if any spies were about. Tom's answer being satisfactory, he said, 'I have come a long way to-night to hear your decision. Tom, we will hear from you.'

"Tom came forward and said in a firm voice, 'I cannot consent to this rising. It can do no good. True, word comes all the way from Virginia and Missouri that if we will commence here where there are few white folks, we can make a good start, and soon an army will fill the land and nothing can stand before us; but, my friends, it isn't so. We can do nothing to better our condition;' and after repeating a part of the Sermon on the Mount he sat down.

"Then the stranger came forward. He was very black, his face shone in the light of the fire. He stood like a statue, his eyes turned towards the heavens for so long a time that the silence seemed painful. Then the tears started from his eyes; he commenced in low, musical tones, 'It's all over, no man will stand by me! God help us! 'He then began to speak of the injustice of slavery, the cruelties, the licentiousness, the degradation, and such impassioned eloquence I never heard from any man as he exhibited when in his final appeal he called upon them to avenge themselves even though there were no hopes of success. He then walked away in another direction from whence he came.

"When he was gone, Tom arose and said, 'Vengeance is mine, I will repay, saith the Lord. I hear that a great many white people pray that God will come down and deliver us, and he will come sure. Let us pray.' They all knelt while Tom prayed, not for the destruction of their enemies, but that they might repent and deliver the poor slaves from bondage. I came away before he closed his prayer."

The next morning, about two hours before daylightour train crossed the Cattaraugus creek on the ice, carrying Jim and his companions towards Canada. Mr. Frink was up and saw the fugitives start, and about sunrise he left for home. When passing a watering trough at the west end of the village, a man was there letting his horse drink. The man spoke to Mr. Frink, and said, "Do you live here, sir?" "No," said Mr. Frink, "Are you acquainted about here?" "Yes," replied Mr. Frink. "Well, can you tell me if there are any abolitionists in this town?" "There may be," said Mr. Frink, "though I could hardly tell who they are. My brother says, 'we are all Democrats here.' " Mr. Frink had mistrusted the fellow at first sight, and the slave catcher, for it was he, thought, no doubt, that Frink was not an abolitionist, else he would know more about it than he seemed to, so he told his business and offered to pay him handsomely if he would help find the fugitives. "Which way did you come?" said Frink. "From the village of Fredonia," was the reply. "I hired this horse there, and supposed I was on the right track, but have not been able to trace the fugitives anywhere this side of that town."

"Did you call on Dr. J. Pettit?"

"No: where does he live?"

"Just out of town, about a mile from where you got your horse. He is a man that would interest himself in your affairs, and could obtain for you more information than all the rest of the people between here and his place."

After getting particular directions so as to find the Doctor's place, the slave hunter thanked Mr. Frink, turned about and drove with all speed, but it was noon when he reined up in front of the said Doctor's house. He was soon seated by the hospitable old fire-place, and without waiting to get warm he made his business known, and asked if the Doctor could ascertain and let him know anything about where to look for the fugitives; "for," said he, "I traced them to a place a mile or two west of here, since which I can hear nothing about them." The Doctor was some time getting a full description of them and then said, "I think I know pretty near where they are now." "Well," said he, brightening up, "you will do me a great favor." "Well," said the Doctor, "they left here about noon yesterday, and I calculate they are crossing the river at Black Rock about this time." "Ah! ah! that is the kind of information you are so well prepared to give." The scene closed with some tall Southern profanity, which was cut short by a request from the lady of the house; she desired him to warm himself as soon as possible and retire, for she did not like to have the children listen to such language.

By the next stage he went to Buffalo, but he was too late, Jim and the boys were safe under the protection of the British Lion.

Jim and his companions were brought from Westfield in a sleigh drawn by Mr. Knowlton's splendid team. They turned off the main road on the West Hill in Fredonia, and changed cars at Dr. P's station in Cordova.

CHAPTER XIV.BLACKSMITH HENRY—WORKS HIS WAY FROM NEW ORLEANS TO BALTIMORE WRITES HIS OWN PASS AND GETS ON TO SPRINGVILLE, N. Y.—FALLS INTO GOOD HANDS AND GETS SAFELY THROUGH—SOME ACCOUNT OF HIS EARLY LIFE—A CHRISTIAN LADY IN KENTUCKY—A PREACHER IN A TIGHT PLACE.

Not many years ago I spent a Sabbath in Springville, Erie Co., N. Y., where I met an old friend, Deacon E——, a zealous worker in the interest of the U. G. R. R. He recalled the case of Henry Rankin, as one of the most interesting fugitives who ever came this way. Henry had been a slave in Kentucky and was a good blacksmith; his master allowed him to find work for himself by paying $30 per month for his time. His master had also agreed to emancipate Henry on the payment of $1,500 out of his extra earnings. Henry paid the stipulated sum, $30, at the close of every month, and on Christmas day he paid over to his master all the money he had left of his extra wages after paying for a good plain suit of clothes with which to commence the new year. Henry was a strong man and an excellent mechanic, and found time after the close of work hours to devote to the acquisition of an education. He became a good reader and writer, and thoroughly understood all the rules in the common arithmetic; he read his bible histories and such other useful books as he could procure

When Henry was twenty-eight years old, he had paid nearly the whole of the stipulated sum to his master and was anxiously looking forward to the next Christmas as the day on which he was to have his free papers, but before that day the old man died, and as, by the laws of the State of Kentucky, no contract made with or by a slave was valid, the heirs refused to acknowledge Henry's claim, although he was prepared to pay the small balance due. They also seized him and sent him to the

New Orleans market where such mechanics as he was would sell for from $3,000 to $5,000.

It was a hard case for poor Henry, but he never gave up the hope of obtaining his freedom, and watching his opportunity he managed to escape on a vessel, on which he had worked making repairs at New Orleans. When the ship was in the Gulf of Mexico, four or five days out, he was discovered on board. The captain and crew respected him for his industry and good behavior as well as for his excellent workmanship as a mechanic; therefore they did not betray him at Baltimore where they landed him, but gave him as good counsel as they could in relation to his best route to Canada. He had some money, and providing himself with a pass written by himself, he left Baltimore and traveled sometimes in the day and sometimes in the night until he came into this State, near Bradford, Pa. Passing the Alleghany Reservation, near Great Valley, thence by the way of Ellicottville, he arrived at Springville one evening and went into a hotel. There was some kind of a gathering there and the bar-room was full of men, so Henry went to the landlord and said, "Please, sir, can you tell me, is there a praying Christian about here?" "Yes," said the landlord, "there is one just around the corner."

"Here, George, show this man where Deacon E—— lives."

The Deacon was the first man to whom Henry had confided his history since he left the ship in Baltimore. He landed safely in Canada, since which we have no account of him, but we have no fears as to his conduct and success as a citizen of his adopted country. Henry escaped from slavery about the time the U. G. R. R. was first organized, and before the lines were all arranged hence he worked his way without aid until he arrived almost in sight of Canada.

The New York *Tribune* quoted from the *Mobile Sunday Times* of July 12th, 1868, an article in which the editor, a rebel Democrat, made the following admission: "The negro population, who are easily led away by novelty and excitement, and extravagant promises, are very *quick to perceive where their vital interests lie,* and to return to the path of common sense when they make the discovery." On reading the above article one morning, I was reminded of a conversation I had with a gentleman in Carlisle, Nicholas Co., Kentucky, which directly corroborated Henry's story. I had stopped one evening at the hotel in said town; at the table a gentleman sat opposite to me whose face and voice seemed familiar. After dinner he came into the public room and sat down near to us, (my brother was with me) and said, "Gentlemen, you are from the North. May I ask what State?" "New York," I answered "Ah! "said he, "I thought so; from the town of Fabius, Onondaga Co. I was sure I had seen you before; your name is Pettit." "Yes," said I, "and you are Frank Chapel, of Pompey. You taught the school in our town when I was a boy." After cordial greeting and congratulations on having met each other so far away from the scenes of our boyhood, he invited us to meet him at his office in the evening.

Chapel had studied law and gone to Kentucky some ten years previous to the time I met him. His talents, general manners and brilliant conversational powers had drawn about him troops of friends and a thriving business. In the evening we fell into conversation on the manners, customs and institutions peculiar to that country, the marked distinction between the wealthy and the slave-holding classes, and the poor class of whites, and the influence of their system of slave labor in producing these distinctions. He related much of what he had witnessed and heard himself, but nothing amused and interested us so much as what he told us of the experience and adventures of a young clergyman with whom he fell in company at Pittsburgh, Pa. He was going to Cynthiana, Ky., where he was expecting to settle. They traveled together and became not only acquainted, but interested in each other's success, just entering, as they both were, into society so different from that in which they had been educated. On the subject of slavery they had never thought or cared much, but they had an impression that negroes were created expressly for slaves; that as to their capacity for the attainment of knowledge and science and the enjoyment of civilized life and social comforts and pleasures, there was no comparison between them and even the most ignorant and degraded of the white race. Therefore, they argued that slavery was the normal condition of the negro.

Although Cynthiana is not more than twenty-five miles from Carlisle, it so happened that Chapel and Rev. Mr. Platt, the clergyman above mentioned, did not meet until about a year after they came together into the State. Chapel was attending court in Harrison Co., of which Cynthiana is the county seat, and called on Mr. Platt to renew their acquaintance. He met with a cordial reception, and was invited to spend his evenings with the reverend gentleman. In the course of the evening Chapel said, "Mr. Platt, how does this slave question affect you? It is a matter of no small moment, at least I find it so." "Well," said Piatt, "I'll tell you I had my eye teeth cut on that question the day I arrived here. You see I had letters of introduction to Mr. Hamilton, a planter (or farmer as he said) living two miles from town. I went immediately to his place, was cordially entertained by the ladies of the family, but Mr. Hamilton was not then at home. Mrs. Hamilton said, 'you will please make this your home until he returns, which will be in three or four days.' I soon discovered that Mrs. Hamilton was a lady of superior talents, refinement and education, a devoted Christian, while m her conversation that which you would notice first was her sound common sense and conscientious honesty of purpose. In the afternoon the ladies, except Mrs. Hamilton, had gone out for a ride, and there were only Mrs. Hamilton and the small children with me in the parlor. The common topics of conversation being exhausted and having seen some slaves about the house, I thought it might be a good time to place myself on the right sort of a platform on the slave question, inasmuch as I came from Massachusetts, where, in some sections of the State, the subject was being agitated. (This was soon after the beginning of the agitation and before the fugitive slave law was thought of) What I said I cannot remember, for what followed obliterated from my mind not only the language I used, but the sentiment that my words expressed. I only recollect that I desired to make Mrs. Hamilton understand that I fully appreciated the beautiful arrangement of Providence in creating a people capable of appreciating the social comforts and intellectual enjoyments of our advanced civilization, with the hopes and the happiness of the Christian religion, and in relieving us of the labor necessarily attendant upon such a state of things by giving us possession of a race of beings not only incapable of such enjoyments, but whose minds and bodies were exactly adapted to the performance of the labor and drudgery needed by us. I am not sure that I had any doubt as to the truth of all this, until on looking up I saw depicted on her countenance grief, astonishment and disgust all combined. It was now my turn to be astonished. I had intended to close with a peroration upon the curse of Canaan, but that was all lost. A glance of her eye paralyzed my tongue. I wished to apologize, but could not do even that. There was silence, and I suffered more in five minutes than I can describe. I thought I saw in her countenance all kinds of emotion, until finally that of pity seemed to predominate.

"Mrs. Hamilton was, I judge, about the age of my mother," said Platt, "and in person, voice and expression, commanding the utmost respect. I have never been able to account for my folly in being so forward in the expression of sentiments that I did not understand, nor did I know whether I believed them or not. After a most painful silence, she was the first to speak, and said, 'My dear sir, when I heard that you were coming here from a New England home, I did hope and expect to hear from you sentiments very different from those you have just expressed. Yet, if such is your view of things on this subject, I am glad to know it now and to have the opportunity to give such advice as a mother might venture to give her son. People from the North are never under a greater mistake than when they suppose that they command the respect of slaveholders by advocating principles such as I have just listened to. Had my husband heard what you have said to me, he might, from courtesy or motives of policy, have seemed to coincide with your views in some measure, but his feelings towards you would have been characterized with the utmost contempt. You will pardon me, sir, for in this plain speaking I put it more mild than the case will warrant. Mr. Hamilton is a man of the world, a slaveholder, and while he regrets the existence of slavery, he says no way has yet been devised by which we can be rid of it, and I doubt not he likes to hear Northern men talk as you do sometimes, for thereby he knows that, politically, the South gets the advantage of the North.

" 'As to the capacity of the negroes, I will relate what I heard Mr. Hamilton say, in conversation with a neighbor on the subject of repealing the laws that prohibit their education. The man pretended to believe as you have said, that they are too ignorant and stupid to learn if they had a chance. My husband said in answer' 'They are ignorant of course; our laws have made them so, and keep the most of them in that condition; but if they are too stupid to avail themselves of a chance for improvement, what is the use of making laws to prevent them from getting an education? No sir; I tell you they have intellects naturally as bright as the white race. Indeed, the whole mass of slaves in Kentucky, with all their disabilities as to education, the degradation and oppression necessarily attending their condition, are, in point of intellect, ahead of the poor whites that are scattered all over the slave States, a disgrace to our civilization; yet *each white man holds a vote* of equal power with the proudest aristocrat in the nation. If the slaves were set free, and I wish to God they were, and placed on an equal footing with the class I spoke of, the blacks would start with a bound on the race of improvement, outstripping the poor whites in the race. I will give you a practical illustration:

" 'The State of Kentucky passed a school law and created a fund for this class of white children, but they never availed themselves of it. Not a common schoolhouse has been built because they never asked for one, and finally the school fund was appropriated to other objects; whereas, not only the law makes it a penal offense to teach a negro, *free* or *slave*, to read, but subjects the negro to a public whipping for trying to learn; yet there are more slaves in this county who can read and write than there are of that class of whites. Yes sir, if made free to-day, the blacks would use the elective franchise more intelligently than they. Why sir,' said he, becoming excited by his own talk, 'there are ten men in the legislature of this State that are not as capable of making laws for the government of the State as my Ben is. His education is better than theirs—the Lord knows how he obtained it—and he has better common sense; and Rankin, there is your blacksmith Henry. Where can you find a better mechanic, or a man better fitted to discharge the duties of a free citizen than he is?'

" 'I give you this,' said Platt, 'as the substance of what she said, in a conversation in which I took some part.'

"I have only to add," said Chapel, "that my observation corroborates all the sentiments expressed by Mrs .and Mr. Hamilton, and," said he, "I believe that nearly all the better portion of the people hold similar opinions, though few will speak as freely on the subject as did Mrs. Hamilton. Platt was thoroughly cured of his toadyism."

From Carlisle we went to Cynthiana, where it was our good fortune to become acquainted with Mr. Hamilton, and we accepted his invitation to visit him at his home. He had buried his good wife some years before, but he wished to introduce us to his son. The father and son were both enthusiastic admirers of Northern institutions, especially our common schools, internal improvements and free labor, and said that Kentucky needed only these to make it the paradise of the United States.

CHAPTER XV. JOE AND ROSA—SOLD—THE ESCAPE—THEY REACH THE SOUTHERN TERMINUS OF U. G. R. R.—DANGER SIGNALS—THE QUAKER FRIEND—THE MASTER ON THE TRACK—OUTWITTED BY THE QUAKER—SAFE IN WILBERFORCE COLONY.

In the Shenandoah Valley, near the Blue Ridge, two slaves, a man and his wife, sat talking late in the evening. They were in trouble, and knew not what to do, and there was not a being on earth to whom they dared to apply for counsel. Both wept and both offered a silent prayer to Him whose ear is ever open to the cry of the poor. Finally the man aroused himself and spoke in low, earnest tones. He said, "Rosa, we must go; I can't bear to see you sold and drove like a beast, in a coffle to the rice swamps of Georgia, to say nothing of myself." She answered, "It can't be possible that master has sold us; we have served him so faithfully for thirty years and always obeyed him. Oh dear, Joe, what shall we do. They will catch us and whip us almost to death, and then we shall be separated never to see each other again. It may be we're not sold, and if we run off he'll sell us sure." Joe answered, "He sold us to-day; I heard him read the names of ten of us, to the trader that has been about here three or four days, and *our names were first*. Yes, Rosa, we must go. If they catch us it can be no worse. The whipping will not be half as hard to bear as the thought that we never tried to be free, and if we die as Sally did when they caught her and whipped her to death for killing the dog that caught her, even that is better than to be driven and sold away from each other."

Fearing that they might be put in jail the next morning, they started about midnight, taking nothing with them, traveling in the road until it began to be light, when they went into a swamp and waded in creeks and swamps until almost noon, so as to baffle the dogs. Then going as near the road as they thought would be safe, they rested until dark, when they started again. Before morning they were so faint from hunger and fatigue that Rosa could go no farther; the next day Joe found some berries and brought to her these and a few roots, and some hours of sleep revived her so that they went forward. The fourth night they became so exhausted by hunger and fatigue that they laid down in the woods expecting to die there, but after resting a while Joe determined to obtain food for his wife at all hazards, and having slept until evening, he left her and went in search of a house. Coming to a road he followed it until he found that he had passed a house. Having the superstition common among slaves, he feared bad luck if he turned back, and so he went on and soon came to another house and knocked at the door. A man opened the door, and looking at Joe, said, "You are a fugitive slave, but be not afraid, come in." It was with great effort that Joe stepped into the house and sat down. The man spoke kindly to him, and when he learned which way he came, he said, "It is well for you that you did not stop at the house you came past; they would have betrayed you. What can I do for you?" Joe could only say "bread." When it was given to him he looked at it and turned it over, seeming as the man thought, to almost devour it with his eyes. He said, "You are starved; why don't you eat?" "Yes," said Joe, "I am starved, but hungry as I am, I could not eat this if I had none for my wife." "Eat," said the man, and going into another room he brought some bread and meat and sent him away, saying, "Stay where your wife is to-night and to-morrow; come here again in the evening. Meanwhile, you must remember that your master will be looking for you. If I see any danger I will warn you by the 'crack of my rifle.'"

When Joe started to go again to the house of their friend, Rosa went with him and stopped behind some bushes near the road. Joe had been gone about ten minutes when she heard horses coming, and looking through the bushes, she saw her master and two of his neighbors go by;

Joe had heard them also, and ran into the woods and soon heard the crack of a rifle. Later in the evening he went again to the house of their friend, who said, "Your master was here an hour ago and asked if I had seen two runaway niggers. I told him that a man and a woman went by pretty fast, but I did not see their faces, and did not know whether they were runaways or not, and he and his men rode off down the road."

Joe and Rosa were in safe hands. They had, through great suffering, hunger, fright and fatigue, been guided by a kind Providence to the Southern terminus of the U. G. R. R. The track had but just reached this point and was not yet in good running order. However, although the trains ran slow and with caution, they were landed safely in Chester Co., Pa., about ten days after they left the first station.

Joe and Rosa found employment in the service of an honest Quaker farmer, who never asked them from whence they came. When they had been there almost a year, the Quaker returned from market one evening and sent for Joe to come to his room. When he came in the farmer said to him, "Be seated, Joseph, I wish to talk with thee. Thee will be careful what thee says; if what I have heard about thee and thy wife be true, thee need not say so, nor is it necessary for thee to deny it. I have found that thou art discreet, and can be silent when to speak truth might result in something unpleasant. A man who says his name is Ridgley, and that he lives in Virginia, is stopping in Chester, and has employed a man who does little else than to hunt fugitives from slavery, to find and arrest a man and a woman that he says escaped from his plantation last year. I overheard the hunter describing them when I went for my horses into the barn this afternoon. The description answered so well to thee and thy wife that I fear he will arrest thee whether ye are the people they are looking for or not. Ye have been faithful servants, and I shall add something to the wages we agreed upon. Now go and talk with thy wife, and then come to me again for thy money, as I do not like to have accounts for labor run too long." The poor fugitive and his wife felt this new trouble severely; they could not understand why two honest, industrious people, who had done no wrong, should be driven from place to place while their persecutors were protected by the government and by society in thus depriving them of their rights. When Joe went again to the farmer Rosa went with him. He gave to them their money, and then said: "Friend Walton starts at ten o'clock this evening so as to be in Philadelphia before morning with his butter; he goes in the night because the days are too warm for the butter. There is a man to whom he will introduce you, and of whom you may buy such clothing as you need at fair prices; his name is Benjamin Harrison. Thee can confide in him with safety, and Joseph, if thee thinks best to relate to him what I have told thee, he will give thee sound advice and efficient aid, but if thee would choose to stay with us, go early to the hay field to work." Walton was a shrewd conductor, and he delivered them at Harrison's U. G. R. R. station in Southwark, a suburb of the Quaker City, in due time.

The following day, about noon, Ridgley called at the house of the Quaker, and as dinner was ready he was invited to partake. He sat down with the family and soon entered into conversation about the fugitives. He spoke of them as having been frightened without cause and run off. They had always been well used, happy and contented, and he had no doubt they would be glad to go back among their friends, as he would assure them they should not be punished if they would go without making him trouble. He had heard that two negroes answering the description of his were living there, and as the people in the neighborhood had long been opposed to the return of fugitives, and might try to prevent their being carried back by process of law, he would like to see them, and if he was not mistaken about their identity, he believed they would rejoice to see him and go home willingly. He asked to have them called in without being told that he was there, that the family might witness their happiness on seeing their old master.

The farmer said that his people were in the hay field at some distance from the house. "Thee will rest here until they come, and I will have them all come in and see if thee can identify them," he added, meanwhile drawing Ridgley into conversation on the subject of slavery, maintaining that the white race had no better right to enslave the blacks than the blacks to enslave the whites. "I am aware," said Ridgley, "that your people are opposed, honestly, no doubt, to our institution, but it exists among us, and must always be so, for should the mad schemes of the abolitionists prevail, amalgamation with all its disgusting results would be sure to follow; and then so numerous a body of ignorant men having the rights of franchise and social position denied them cannot be controlled in any other position than that in which they are now held."

"As to amalgamation," said the Quaker, "I regard emancipation as the only possible method of putting a stop to it; for when both races are left to their own free choice the practice ceases. It has always been so and will be no different hereafter. The laws never interfere in such matters when all parties are free. Slavery forces amalgamation; it is not in practice among free men. What thou sayest in relation to the difficulty in controling so large a body of ignorant men, having their rights denied them, is without foundation, for when they are free they will not long remain in ignorance, and as to the right of franchise, if they cannot be made good citizens without it, then why deprive them of it?" "Why deprive them?" said Ridgley, "they are deprived of it already!" "True," said the Quaker, "slaves do not vote, but when slavery is abolished they will be citizens, and if to make them voters will make them better citizens, more easily governed because aiding in the government, then I say, why not grant them equal rights?" "Because," said Ridgley, "we should soon be overrun by them? Who would ever consent to be ruled by niggers?" "It seems to me," said the Quaker, "that thee puts a low estimate on the capacity of the white race to maintain republican institutions if thee believes what thee says, that with equal rights twenty millions of whites cannot compete with four millions of black men; thy self-respect must suffer serious damage in the contemplation of such conclusions. 'I noticed that among the rights of which thee takes it for granted that black men, after emancipation, will be deprived, thee has classed what thee calls 'social position.' In that thou art mistaken; social position is not a right of which free men can be deprived by law, it is a condition to which men attain, or fail in the attainment, by conduct, talents and energy. In no other nation except this does the attainment of high social position depend on the color of the skin, and here, secure to him his freedom and equal rights before the law and the black man in his struggle for social position will willingly bide his time."

"Well," said Ridgley, "I have not time now to answer all you have said, and to be honest I am constrained to acknowledge that the black man, even in slavery, does not occupy the lowest grade to which men are capable of going. We have, at the South, a class of low, white trash that Joe and Rosa would scorn to associate with."

When the "hands" came in from the hay field, Ridgley looked among them in vain for his lost chattels, although there were among them colored men and women.

"Are these all?" said Ridgley. "Jacob," said the Quaker to his foreman, "where are Joseph and Rosa?" "They went to the city this morning," was the reply; "they had a chance to ride, and as they wanted some clothes, I thought they had better go, and we have finished the having without their help," The countenances of the colored people present betrayed them. Ridgley saw at once that his chattels had been too smart for him, and taking a hasty leave of the shrewd Quaker's family, whom he hardly suspected of being active agents on the U. G. R. R., he hastened towards Philadelphia, but he was never so near to them again as he was the night he stayed in Chester. Joe and Rosa passed through the old headquarters of the institution at Albany; at Syracuse Rev. J. W.

Loguen gave them letters to leading men in the Wilberforce Colony, C. W., and tickets by steamer across Lake Ontario.

Mr. S——, one of the leading men in Wilberforce Colony, was at our house a few years after the above scenes transpired, and mentioned Joe and Rosa as among the most successful farmers and respectable citizens in the settlement.

CHAPTER XVI.CASSEY ESCAPES FROM BALTIMORE—RETURNS FOR HER CHILD—ESCAPES AGAIN IN SAILOR COSTUME—ELUDES THE SLAVE CATCHER, CATHCART—GOES TO CANADA—RETURNS TO NIAGARA FALLS, N. Y.—THE SLAVE CATCHER FINDS HER—A LONG RIDE AND HOW IT CAME OUT—AN INTELLIGENT IRISHMAN—WHAT MARGARET DID FOR HIM.

Cassey was a slave in Baltimore; her master's name was Claggett. She had been assured by those who knew, that she was about to be sold to a man who was making up a coffle for the markets in Louisiana or Texas. None but slaves can imagine the terror felt in view of such a prospect. Cassey fled like a frightened bird, and succeeded in reaching a place of safety near Haddonfield, N. J., where she obtained service in a respectable family. She was industrious, steady and honest, and her cheerful, obliging manners secured her many friends, yet a sadness was ever present on her countenance, for she had left in Baltimore a child, little more than a year old. Her master had not been unusually severe, but she had experienced and witnessed enough of slavery to dread it for her child, and she therefore determined to make a desperate effort to save her little one from the liability of being sold and treated like a mere brute. The kind Quaker people among whom she had found a home tried to dissuade her from attempting so hazardous an enterprise, deeming it not only dangerous, but well nigh hopeless; but the mother's heart yearned for her babe, and she finally decided to try to save it at all hazards.

She went to Baltimore and proceeded directly to the house of a colored family, old friends of hers, in whom she could safely confide. To her great joy she found that they approved her plan and were ready to assist her. Arrangements were soon made to convey the child to a place about twenty miles from Baltimore, where it would be well taken care of until the mother could safely take it to New Jersey.

Before she could leave the city her master was informed that she was there and sent constables in pursuit of her, but her friends were apprized of it in season to give her warning, and her own courage and ingenuity were adequate to the emergency. She disguised herself in sailor's clothes and walked boldly to the Philadelphia boat. There she walked up and down the deck smoking a cigar, occasionally passing and re-passing the constables who had been sent to take her. The constables left the boat after waiting till it was about to start; they were watching for a colored woman to come on board answering to her description. The boat brought her safely to Philadelphia, and she soon reached her friends in Haddonfield, who rejoiced over the history of her escape and the success of her enterprise. A few weeks after she went to the place where her child had been left, and succeeded in bringing it away in safety.

For a short time her happiness seemed to be complete; but she soon began to be harassed with fears that her master would succeed in finding them and take them both back to slavery. At length she resolved to go to Philadelphia, which was not far distant, and get the advice of Benjamin Harrison, a Quaker who was ever ready to aid fugitives from slavery. He advised her to leave her child in the care of a family living quite remote from public travel, where it would be entirely safe, and go herself farther north. Acting upon friend Harrison's advice, she had placed her child in the care of the family that he recommended and returned to Philadelphia, intending to start north in a day or two; but, passing along the street in which her friend lived, she met Cathcart, the speculator to whom she had been sold. Hurrying forward she reached the door of her friend in time to go in before he could get hold of her. Harrison saw the chase and locked his doors. Cathcart placed men about the house to watch while he went for constables and a warrant. It was evening, and the offices being closed, he was slow in obtaining his papers; meanwhile, in passing through his kitchen, Harrison saw that two of his domestics seemed very merry over some project they had on foot, and he watched their movements. One of them put on an old cloak and a dilapidated bonnet, and opening the front door looked up and down the street; then rushing out she turned a corner and ran with all her might. The watchers saw it all, sprang from their hiding places and overtook her. She screamed and called for the police, who soon arrived and took all parties into custody. During the excitement Cassey escaped, and before Cathcart returned with his constables she was crossing the Delaware River in a skiff. She was so terribly frightened by this adventure that she determined not to stop again short of Canada. Having saved her earnings she was able to travel by steamboat and canal packet, and soon arrived in Canada and found friends and a home at Lundy's Lane, near Niagara Falls.

Cassey's boy was a fine, active little fellow, and she determined to earn money to buy his freedom, for, being a very capable woman, she commanded high wages. The agent of the U. G. R. R., at Niagara Falls, was a wealthy gentleman, living some two miles back from the river, where he had an excellent farm, a fine mansion, splendid stock and superb horses. All the negro servants at the Falls were in the secret service of the institution, and not a few of the white citizens were friendly toward it. When Cassey had been in Canada three or four years our agent above mentioned applied to her to engage in his service, and as he would pay her much higher wages than she could obtain in Canada, she, supposing that all danger had passed, came over on the Suspension Bridge and went to work for him. She never went into the village except to go occasionally to meeting on Sunday. One Sunday, as she passed out of the church, she saw a man standing near the door, sharply scanning the features of every colored person that came out.

Her eyes met his and they recognized each other, but she managed to get away in the crowd and he lost sight of her.

The facilities offered by the fugitive slave law for capturing runaway slaves had made it a profitable business, and Cathcart had bought "running" a large lot of fugitives, expecting to make a good speculation if he could capture even one in ten of them. He had come on to the Falls, rightly guessing that some of them would be about there, and he was at the church door in pursuit of his regular business. One of the shrewdest men, either white or black, that lived in that village, was Ben Jackson, a free negro. Ben was a servant in the hotel where Cathcart was stopping, and he had already, as was his custom, taken pains to talk with other colored servants in Cathcart's presence about the slaves running away and coming here to work for almost nothing, saying, "we 'spectable niggers can't get anything to do half the time, and we get drefful little for it when we get a place. They ought to be tuck back where they belong." Cathcart went directly to Ben, and taking him aside, he described Cassey, told where he saw her, and inquired if Ben knew her. "Yes," said Ben, "I knows her. She lives over to Lundy's Lane. She comes over on the Suspension Bridge sometimes to Methodist meeting." Cathcart had already engaged a score of shaggy Democrats to start at his bidding, and he sent two of them without delay to watch the bridge, and others were sent to all the crossing places between Tonawanda and Youngstown, the gate-keeper at the bridge having told him that no such person had crossed over to Canada that day.

Ben lost no time in sending word to Cassey and to Col. P——, with whom she lived, telling them how he had misled the slave hunter. As soon as it was dark a trusty conductor started with Cassey towards Lockport, and Col. P had his fleetest team harnessed to a close carriage, standing in his barn ready to start at a moment's warning.

Cathcart came back from the bridge, and calling the landlord aside, told him that he had seen one of the slaves that he was looking for; he also related what Ben had said to him. "Well," said the landlord, "Ben is a trusty fellow generally, but you ought to know better than to confide in any negro on business relating to fugitives." "But I heard him saying that the runaway niggers were working for low wages and ought to be sent back." "Ben said that," replied the landlord, "when he knew you would hear it. Did the woman recognize you?" "I think she did," said Cathcart. "Then," said the landlord, "no time is to be lost. She has no doubt gone to Col. P . He has wealth and influence, and whatever you do with him must be done legally. You have the law and the strongest party in the State on your side, while he knows just how much or how little the law can do for you. He has at his command means for hiding and running off these people that no one has yet found out. They call it the Underground Railroad. *They must go under ground or by balloon,* for once in his hands they are never seen again this side of the river." The President had not been so careless of the interests of his slaveholding friends who visit the Falls as to leave them without the means of reclaiming their fugitive servants. A Commissioner and Marshals were located there, so that Cathcart, although it was Sunday evening, had his papers in the Marshal's hands as soon as possible, and he, with his deputies, were by ten o'clock, p. m., approaching Col. P——'s place by different roads. Meanwhile, the Colonel had his spies out, and he was on the front seat of his carriage, with his driver, in his barn. When the Marshal drew near, a signal was given, the barn door opened suddenly, and the Colonel, with the fastest team in Niagara County, dashed out and down the road toward Lewiston. The Marshal was coming on that road and tried to stop him, but he passed on and was followed by the officers who tried to get ahead. The Colonel tantalized them by allowing them to come alongside, but to get by or to stop him was out of the question. Thus he led them all the way to the ferry at Youngstown, having passed Lewiston without stopping. At Youngstown he allowed them to drive past him, but before the Marshal could get to him he turned about and started back toward home, the officers still keeping in sight of him until he drove into his barn. When he stopped the officers were close by, and rushing up to both sides of the carriage, were astonished to find no person inside of it, the Colonel having been careful to allow them to keep near enough to know positively that no person had left the carriage since it started. "Come into the house, gentlemen, and have some refreshments," said the Colonel. "Bill, rub down their horses, they are a fine team, and have tried the bottom of my grays. I thought you would give it up at Lewiston, but as you decided to go on I thought if any team in this county could show better bottom for a long drive than mine, I should like to know it." By this time the Marshal had made up his mind that there was no game there, and he drove on without waiting for Bill to groom his horses or to hold any conversation with the Colonel.

One of the best conductors in Niagara County was an Irishman by the name of Dennis W——. He lived on a good farm between the canal and the ridge road, about four miles from Lockport. He was active, intelligent and industrious. I first knew him as an active member of the Liberty Party, and afterwards as a conductor on the U. G. R. R. When Col. P found the crossing dangerous, he sent passengers to Dennis, while he managed to mislead the hunters. The conductor who took Cassey to his station, told Dennis not to keep her about his own premises, for he was beginning to be suspected. Dennis had a friend who came from Ireland a year or two previous, and he had fixed up a place for him to live in on a remote part of his farm. Supposing it would be a safe place for Cassey to stop a few days, he went to see if he would take her into his house, and said to him, "Jimmy, I have a favor to ask of you." "Ye shall have it before I know what it is," said Jimmy, "though it might be half of my kingdom!" "It isn't that," said Dennis, "I only want a place for a poor woman to stay a few days." He then told who she was, and gave a thrilling account of her troubles and the terrible things she would have to suffer if she was captured. When he had told her story it had just got into Jim's head that she was a negro, and he exclaimed, "It's a nagur ye would bring here, is it? I'll have none of it! It's the same that's coming here in swarms if they make Linkin and that other nagur President; and won't they work for nothing, and then the poor folks can get no work? and wasn't that what the man said at the Dimicrat meeting up there to Lockport?—and they are coming already, are they? No, no, away wid'em!" When Jimmy had given vent to his feelings and his fears, Dennis said, "I will tell you a short story. You know I came over here twenty-five years ago, and left Mary and her baby to come when I could earn money to send for them. Well, I was sick on the ship, and when I landed in New York I was sick, and had no money and no place to go to. I wandered in the streets too sick to work or to eat, and after a while I think I lost my senses, for I awoke one morning and couldn't imagine where I was.

After a while a woman spoke to me and said, 'are you better? you will get well and go and see Mary.' I said, 'where is Mary?' She replied, 'I don't know. You have talked about her, and I guess she is away in Ireland.' She brought some food and I ate a very little.

The room was dark, so I had not seen her face; when she brought a light I saw that she was as black as a boot. I should have been frightened, but her voice was sweet, and she spoke so tenderly that I did not mind her looks.

"The woman who saved my life was called Margaret. She had been a slave and escaped, bringing off her little boy. She had found me lying on her door-step, almost dead, taken me in and nursed me into life again. When I was well enough to work she kept me until I found work, and then lent me money to send for Mary and the boy. Well, I can't stop now to tell how I prospered and bought this farm, went to school—yes, went to school with children, and when I had been here the proper time I was naturalized, and supposed I was a Democrat and would vote their ticket. At the first election I attended, a man gave me a vote and said, 'you are a Democrat, of course, and here is another vote.' I said, 'what is that?' and looking at it I saw it was something about the Constitution. He said it was to prevent negroes from voting if they had not real estate worth $250, and I said, 'can't Irishmen vote until they have real estate?' 'Oh, yes,' said he, 'but the negroes are ignorant.' Said I, 'the first person that treated me kindly in this country was a black negro, was once a slave, and it took me five years to learn what she knew then of books, and as to general information she was better informed than her white neighbors. Her son, Samuel R. Ward, was an educated gentleman, and I see no reason why he should not vote as well as I. No, sir,' said I, 'if that is Democratic doctrine I can't vote your ticket,' and now I see the same party are at their old tricks. They tell you that black men will do all the work for nothing. It is not because men are black that they work for nothing, but because they are held in slavery. When all men become free citizens labor will command its value."

"What do you say," said Dennis, "shall I bring her here for a few days?"

"Yes," said Jimmy, "let her come, and may the holy Virgin forget me whin I'm in sorest need if I let a spalpeen of a Democrat hurt a hair of her head."

She had been at Jimmy's place but a short time when the rebels fired on our flag, after which Cassey went back and found her boy, and as fugitives were now safe in New Jersey she decided to remain with her Quaker friends.

CHAPTER XVII. TOM HAWKINS—NEGROES AND POOR WHITES IN KENTUCKY—TOM RUNS HIS OWN TRAIN—SELLS HIS SHIRT TO PAY HIS FARE AT THE FERRY—IS BORN INTO GOD'S FREE AIR ALMOST AS NAKED AS HE WAS BORN INTO SLAVERY—HIS MODESTY, INDUSTRY, INTELLIGENCE AND PROSPERITY.

It has been a common belief in the Free States that the slaves in the South were the most ignorant and the most stupid human beings to be found in any country blessed with Christian civilization, and from that idea, mainly, has arisen the fear in the minds of many good people that the Republican doctrine of universal, loyal, manhood suffrage may prove a disastrous experiment. As an offset to such grounds of fear, it may be well to remember that there is a large class of white men living in the midst of the black population in the old slave States, who are even more ignorant, more stupid, and in all respects more degraded than the slaves were, the slaveholders themselves being judges, yet the "poor white trash," as the aristocracy and even the slaves call them, have equal rights at the ballot box with their rich and intelligent neighbors. Since the slaves were emancipated, schools have been established for the benefit of all classes, black and white, of which the blacks almost universally avail themselves, while the aforesaid class of poor whites, with few exceptions, treat every attempt to educate and elevate them with utmost scorn.

When traveling in the slave States twenty years ago, I found this class of white people unable to give any information as to the distance to the nearest town, and not one in ten knew the name of the county where they lived. Between Paris and Winchester, Ky., a heavy shower came upon us, and we found shelter in a house in the edge of the woods. A man and his wife, and five or six children, were in the house, and the combined wisdom of the household could give us no information as to how far it was to either of the above towns. "It was a right smart chance of a walk," and that was all they knew about it, nor did they know the name of the county they lived in, or the political party the "old man" voted for; he thought, however, his name was not "political party." "Was it Harry Clay?" "No, it was t'other feller." When the shower was over we started towards Winchester, and soon met an old negro passing along the road. Stopping our horse, I said, "Good evening, uncle." He took off his hat and responded, "Good ebening, sar." I said, "Put your hat on your head, my friend, you are an old man." He looked at us, then at his hat, and finally put his hat under his arm, and stood uneasily, turning partly around. Seeing that he felt embarrassed, I thought I would ask him some questions, and see if the old negro was as ignorant as the Loco Foco voter whose roof had partially sheltered us during the late shower, so I asked, "How far is it to Winchester?" "Bout four mile." "How far to Paris?" "Ten or twelve mile," he replied, both of which answers proved correct. "Can you tell us what county we are in?" "Dis am Clark County," said he, "but just ober dar is Bourbon County," and pointing west, he said, "dat way, bout two mile, am Fayette County." We found the old slave quite intelligent on many subjects. I asked him where he lived, and he said, "In Fayette County, most down to Lexington. I'se looking forde mules; Massa Hawkins' mules am run off." When we started along he put his hat on, then snatching it off again, he said, "Please, master, do you live down to Louisville?" I answered, "No; why do you wish to know?" "Cause," said he, "my boy Tom was sold down de river, and I hear he cook on steamboat, and come to Louisville sometimes. His old mother wants to hear if he is alive." As we did not live in Louisville, we could give the old man no news to carry to Tom's mother. Whether the old woman ever heard about Tom going ashore near Louisville and getting lost, and not finding his way back again, I do not know, but that such was his fate I have no doubt, nor am I quite sure that his arrival in Canada can be justly credited to the U. G. R. R., for he "paddled his own canoe" and engineered his own train on independent principles.

On the 15th of the present month (September, 1868), I met on the steamboat between Mayville and Jamestown, Dr. C——, a gentleman with whom I had some business transactions in Canada more than twenty years ago. He was then a merchant, and carried on an extensive distillery and ashery at a village some eight or ten miles from St. David's. We did not recognize each other at first, until he incidentally mentioned the name of Hon. Hamilton Merritt, whose wife was the daughter of Mr. P——, one of the first settlers in Jamestown. Recollecting that Mr. Merritt lived in Canada, I asked the gentleman if he had lived there. He answered that he had, and we soon renewed our acquaintance. One of our party asked him if he was acquainted with any of the fugitives who went there. He said he had employed several of them, one of whom was the strongest man he had ever seen. His name was Jack. One day Jack drove to the ashery with a load of wood, and came to the house and asked for a shirt. He had found a negro in the woods who had no clothes except a part of a pair of pants. Jack was a very large man, and his shirts were too large for the fugitive, so he asked for a donation to clothe the poor fellow. A comfortable suit of clothes was soon provided, and Jack brought the boy in with his next load of wood; he was taken to the kitchen, where he was warmed and fed, and at night a comfortable place was provided for him to sleep in. The next morning when the Doctor got up, he found his boots and the shoes and boots of all his family nicely brushed and "shined up," and when he came home at evening he noticed that the wood was all piled in his wood-house in a very orderly manner, and on going to his horse barn and carriage house he found the barn swept and put in order, harnesses and carriages brushed and cleaned, and the poor fugitive was there putting things in order generally. Going up to him, Dr. C—— said, "Who has been meddling with these things?" "Beg pardon," said the boy,

"I had nothing else to do." "Well," said the Doctor, "go into the kitchen and get your supper." On inquiry, he learned that the boy had been busy every moment during the day, though his feet were in a terrible condition, and his body reduced by starvation to a mere skeleton. After tea the boy was invited into the sitting room, and the Doctor said to him, "What is your name?" He replied, "It am Tom Hawkins."

Tom seemed afraid to talk about himself, but the Doctor assured him that he was safe, and that no person could claim him as a slave, and he was finally induced to relate his adventures. He had been a servant on a steamboat on the Mississippi river, and had been kind and serviceable to a passenger who was very sick on the boat. Tom found out that the man might be trusted, and ventured to ask him how he could obtain his freedom. He advised him to secrete himself on a boat that was lying near where they had stopped and keep himself hidden among the freight until they got to Pittsburgh, then showing him the north star and teaching him the way to find it, he told him to go towards it until he came to water that he could not see across, then turn to the right and keep within sight of it until he could see land and houses on the other side; "that," said he, "is Canada. Get over there and you will be a free man."

Tom Hawkins had witnessed more than once cases of excruciating torture inflicted on defenseless, captured fugitives, and knew that just such punishment awaited him if he should fail in an attempt to gain his freedom; but such was his yearning for liberty, the prompting of his untutored manhood, that he did not shrink from the trial. He was so fortunate as to smuggle himself on board a boat that favored his escape as far as Pittsburgh, but when he found himself alone on the north shore of the river, a few miles below the city, without food, except a small supply for a day or two, no clothes except a light summer suit, ignorant of the geography of the country, and of any direct route to a place of safety that seemed to him to exist only in imagination; and worst of all, beholding an enemy, as he supposed, in every human being that he met, in the dreariness of a dark, rainy night in the woods, he thought over the horrid scenes he had been compelled to look upon, of captured fugitives that had been returned to slavery by virtue of the fugitive slave law, and whipped to death as a warning to any who thought of running away. Tom was not discouraged by all this. He sat down and called to mind the instruction his friend gave him about the way to the place where all are free, and determined to follow it out without the least variation; consequently he did not go forward until nearly morning, when the clouds broke and he obtained his bearings by a sight of the north star.

It would be tedious to follow him through long days waiting in the woods, and longer nights when clouds obscured his only guide. He went sometimes in the roads, then in woods or fields, and at length arrived at the ridge of highland south of Erie, Pa., when all at once he looked down upon the "wide water," as it had been described. It was to Tom as if all material things had disappeared, and heaven burst suddenly into view. To him, that beautiful panorama of woods and fields, towns and rural homes, and the broad lake beyond with no shore in sight, was a sure token that all his friend had said to him was true, not only as to the way that he should go, but also regarding the liberty, prosperity and protection that he should enjoy at the end of his perilous journey. So cautious was he that he traveled mostly in fields, woods, and through bushes, living on such corn, vegetables and fruits as he could procure, and when he arrived at the ferry near Lewiston, he had worn out all his clothes except his shirt and pants, and lost his hat. He was sitting near the boat when the ferryman and some passengers came in the morning, and just as they were starting he stepped on board. The boatsman demanded a shilling for his passage, and as he had no shilling he was ordered off the boat, but Tom stripped off his shirt and offered to sell it for a shilling, and finding a purchaser, he paid his fare and went over.

In his extreme caution he had avoided being seen even by our vigilant U. G. R. R. agents, and now found himself born into God's free air almost as naked as he was born into slavery. Hence, as it was early in the morning, he managed to get through the village of Queenstown and into a place where he stayed until evening, when he started along the road, and in the morning laid down exhausted, starved and cold by a pile of wood, where Jack found him and "took him in" as above related. Tom Hawkins proved himself worthy of the freedom he had achieved. It was edifying to witness the enthusiasm of the Doctor in speaking of Tom's capabilities. He employed him as a "man of all work" at $15 per month, high wages for that time. Tom had a "weakness" that stood in the way of financial prosperity, namely, a soft heart toward everybody that wanted to borrow his money,, and so many of these were lazy, dishonest scamps, that at the end of six months he had nothing to show for the wages he had earned except a suit of clothes. The Doctor advised him to take better care of his money, so as to buy him a home. "Well, then," said Tom, "you must keep my money, and when I ask for money to lend to a lazy chap that won't pay, you can just get mad and not let me have it." About that time a man offered for sale fifteen acres of heavily timbered land two miles from town, and the Doctor proposed to Tom to buy it. He hesitated about getting into debt, but Dr. C—— said, "I will take care of that." "Well, then," said Tom, "you know best, master." Tom always persisted in calling him "master." At the end of five years Tom had paid for his land, and bought one of the best teams in the country, and a first rate harness and wagon, and commenced marketing his wood. The Doctor said that one of Tom's peculiarities was that when he purchased anything for his own use he always bought the best that was to be had. An English gentleman living in the town had, in his family, a handsome colored girl. She was well educated, industrious, and a very capable housekeeper, of a sunny temper and agreeable address. Tom built a good house, and then asked this girl to become his wife. They were married, and Tom Hawkins is now regarded as one of the most thrifty farmers in the district. His farm, his house, his barns, and everything that appertains to them are kept in the neatest possible condition, and his note or his word is good for any sum that he would ask for, and I might add that when he became a freeholder in Canada he became a voter. How many white boys with nothing but their hands, their energy, talents and good conduct for capital in starting in the world, can show a better record than Tom Hawkins?

CHAPTER XVIII.WILLIAM AND MARGARET—SEVENTY YEARS OLD AND DETERMINED TO BE FREE—HALF BROTHER TO A U. S. SENATOR—ARGUMENT IN A R. R. CAR.

During an experience of many years in the transactions of the U. G. R. R., no incident is remembered as more sad than the voluntary exile of William Holmes and his wife, Margaret, at about seventy years of age. They arrived at our station late in the evening of a very cold day, and although well protected with blankets and Buffalo robes, they suffered terribly on the route to our station at Versailles from Fredonia, from which station they started at 3 p. m. The snow was deep and much drifted, and it was one of the coldest days of the season. They had seldom seen snow more than a day at a time, and to cross a river on a bridge of ice was an idea that they could not comprehend until they found themselves rising the east bank of the Cattaraugus Creek (the crossing was on the ice, there being no bridge at that time), on the way to friend Andrew's station.

As soon after their arrival as they were fed and comfortably warmed, they went to bed. An hour before daylight they heard a boy making a fire, and Margaret was up and at work before the room was warm. When the family came into the sitting room they found her sweeping, and she insisted upon helping about the work as long as she could find anything to do. She was of medium height, and remarkably well formed for one of her age, and evidently had never been overworked; she was tidily dressed, and her gray hair was nearly concealed under a turban, tastefully arranged. Her voice was low and soft, and her language such as you would hear in good families in the slave States, including their peculiar phrases and provincialisms, such as "a heap," "a right smart chance," etc., etc.

Holmes was a large man. His hair was almost white; his features had none of the peculiarities of the negro, and the complexion of both of them was so nearly white that but for the kink of their hair, few people would suppose they could have been slaves. Margaret was smart and lively as a girl, but William was nearly crippled by rheumatism. Margaret was anxious to assist about ironing, and remarked that she "did not know who would take care of her mistress' nice things now; she had always done it, and she had dressed her ever since she was a child," A sadness came like a cloud on her pleasant face when she spoke of it, but when reminded that in one more day she would be where there was no more slavery, the expression of her countenance was like the sun shining on a beautiful landscape after a summer shower.

Her mistress had been kind to her, punishing her gently for any mistakes or neglect of duty by slapping her face with the sole of her shoe, and sending her to bed without her supper if she cried about it. She knew that Margaret had the blood of her own family in her veins, and that she had been promised her freedom long ago, which promise had been often renewed; that her children had been torn from her and sold, an excuse for so doing being ever at hand, in their temper and complexion, for which reasons, no doubt, she had been lenient in her treatment of her faithful slaves.

William Holmes claimed to be a near relative to his master, whose name he bore, and who was a Senator in the Congress of the United States. He, too, had been promised his freedom, a boon that he had longed for every hour of a long life, until despairing of the fulfillment of the promise, he and his wife, in their old age, resolved to be free in this life and die in a free country, and they availed themselves of an opportunity to make their escape, the details of which they refused to divulge lest their friends might suffer. Their movements at the start were such as to direct attention towards Wilmington, N. C., and before the Senator had given up watching for their embarkation on a Boston ship at that port, they were far on their journey towards Ohio. They started during the Christmas holidays, and their old age and light complexion enabled them to travel without being suspected; besides, I have supposed that some member of the Holmes family, knowing the promises that had been made them, and the injustice and cruelty with which they had been treated in having the promises of their freedom broken and their children sold; knowing also their intense longing for liberty, conducted them through the long route to our station on the Ohio River, for they came that way and had a list of names of the U. G. R. R. agents, including several men of note in Ohio They were both professors of religion, and the spirit of forgiveness, humility and patience, exemplified in the conversation of Margaret, was evidence of true piety, and her gentle rebukes to William when his indignation got the control of his language, was evidence of her care for his spiritual welfare and Christian reputation.

They had so entirely eluded pursuit that all fear of capture had subsided, and they might have remained in safety in our neighborhood, yet their hatred of slavery was such that they would make no long tarry short of a place where slavery was a thing not possible, though they felt safe in spending a few hours with us. It was but six miles to the next station, where they would stay over night, therefore we availed ourselves of the opportunity to get what information we could from our guests.

William was intelligent, and could read and write, had spent many winters in Washington, from whence he would have escaped long ago but for his affection for Margaret and the aforesaid promise of emancipation. He had a calm and dignified manner in speaking on any subject except his own condition, parentage and degradation; on that subject he could not talk without becoming so excited that, notwithstanding his profession of piety, he would swear in a somewhat modified style; then Margaret would chide him in her pleasant way, saying, "Now don't, Willie, it will only make you feel bad to talk so, and I'd a heap rather be in your place than his. Besides, maybe old massa will repent some time." Then he would cool down, and under her eye, talk without excitement a few minutes. Said he: "The man I called master was my half brother. My mother was a better woman than his, and I was the smartest boy of the two, but while he had a right smart chance at school, I was whipped if I asked the name of the letters that spell the name of the God that made us both of one blood. While he was sent to college, I had no teacher but old Pomp, but great pains were taken to teach me that the whole power of the nation was pledged to keep me in slavery. I might protest, threaten, feign sickness or run away, the struggle was against fearful odds, therefore the less we knew the less we would suffer. When we were boys," said he, "I asked him one day when we were playing together, why I might not learn to read as well as he. 'Because,' said he, 'slaves ought not to know too much, it would make them discontented; they know more now than the poor white trash,—I heard father say so'—while I know," said William, "that the 'poor white trash' naturally know as much as the rich white trash, give them both the same advantage in the world." By this time he had become so excited that Margaret found it necessary to soothe him. A few kind, encouraging words from her acted like magic on William's excitable temper, though his temper was the result of a keen sense of wrong, comparing his own condition with that of his half brother.

A friend who now resides in Fredonia was then living in Simcoe, Canada West, and saw William and Margaret a few weeks after they left our station, on their way to the Wilberforce Colony, apparently happy in their new found freedom, and confident in their ability to take care of themselves.

No incident has come under my own observation in a long time that so forcibly reminded me of Holmes' voice, excited manner, and eloquence in appealing to the patriotism and humanity of his audience, like one I witnessed in a car on the Lake Shore Road. Two men were conversing on the prospects of the parties in the present canvass. Sitting near them, I heard one of them, who resembled Holmes in his age, size and physical development, talking low and apparently little excited while the other, who seemed to have the advantage of education and experience in handling the subjects under discussion, persisted in trying to make the financial question, as stated and maintained by the Copperheads, the leading and paramount question to be settled by the present canvass. Whenever the old man tried to introduce the question of reconstruction on loyal principles, or free loyal suffrage, his antagonist would seem not to hear or to notice what he said, but in the noise and confusion I could hear now and then the phrases, "bloated bondholders," "greenbacks," "taxes," "national debt," &c., &c. A crowd gathered around them, one of whom is a peddler, who is always on every train. From him you would hear "nigger voters," "nigger equality," ringing the changes on the "nigger" all the way up to marrying somebody's wife or daughter.

The old gentleman held his own manfully, though I could not understand all that was said, until, finding himself beset on all sides by a pack of noisy Democrats, he stood up and taking the attitude that reminded me of the old man Holmes, in a voice not very loud, but so distinct that half the people in the car heard him, he said, "Gentlemen, this talk about financial ruin, repudiation of honest debts, contrivances to make our government odious and our people the cowardly, dishonest knaves the rebels claim they are, may all seem profitable and pleasant to you, but when you ask me to vote for the red-handed devils, or any who sympathize with them, that murdered, in malice aforethought, 50,000 prisoners, starved my own boy until there was not a pound of flesh on his bones, and then shot him on their 'dead line' when reaching across to get a little water, in the only place where water was to be had, water, for which he had been famished through a long day, I beg to be excused."

"Then," said he, "in order to belittle these vital issues? your Seymours and Pendletons are stretching out long lines of figures with the sign of dollars at the head to frighten the people into choosing rulers who make dollars their god, and loyalty a thing to be bought and sold," and turning to the man who had been ringing changes on this financial question, he said, "Who are the men, which is the party that has heaped this burden of debt upon this nation? Let's hear from you on that!" By this time the man had learned that equivocation wouldn't go far in the controversy, and declined answering. "Well," said the old man, "after bringing this burden of taxation into the house, you propose to disown your own offspring."

Then turning toward the aforesaid peddler, who had stood their grinning during the old man's talk, he said, "I think you made some remark about the Republican going *down to the level of the negro*. Now, sir, it may be of use for you to know that if you ever get on to that level, you will be going *up* instead of *down,* and I advise you to take it moderately, for it would make your head swim to go up all at once."

CHAPTER XIX.AN OLD TIME MISSIONARY AT THE SOUTH— SPEAKS HIS MIND BUT LOSES HIS SHIRTS—THE SLAVEHOLDER'S PENITENT LETTER.

One of the early settlers in Onondaga Co., N. Y., was Rev. Mr. R——. He was a highly educated clergyman, and a popular preacher. The church in the rural township of F——, where he owned one of the best farms in the county, would have been glad to secure his services as pastor, but having property sufficient to maintain his family, and a wife who was capable of managing his affairs, he determined to devote himself to missionary labor in the far South. No recollections of my childhood are more vividly and distinctly marked in my memory than his portly figure, firmly seated in his saddle on his great chestnut mare, with immense saddle bags stuffed to their utmost capacity with changes of linen, children's toy books, tracts and Testaments, and the dfelight with which, after an absence of half a year, all the children in the settlement greeted his return, and listened to his wonderful stories of his adventures, missionary labors and providential escapes from wild beasts in the wilderness and alligators in the rivers. When he described the growing cotton, indigo, rice and sugarcane, it seemed to us children that he must have been half around the world since we saw him last. There were in those days no missionary societies, therefore he was self-appointed and self-sustained, paid his own expenses, thought his own thoughts and spoke his own opinions, which were not always quite agreeable to his slaveholding brethren. There being as yet no abolition excitement, he met with little trouble. Whatever cruelty might have been practiced toward the slaves, little of it came under his observation, but in trying to do his duty to all classes, the poor and the rich, the bond and the free, the degradation of the low order of the white population became a source of astonishment and grief to him, and the slaves, who seemed both more intelligent and more happy than they, so far as he had observed, occupied an enviable position in comparison.

Being in Charleston, S. C., one day, he bought material for some shirts, intending to stop a day and get them made at brother Poindexter's, a Baptist brother, living on his plantation farther down. Before he got out of the city, he heard, in passing a large building, an auctioneer selling property, while his voice was almost drowned by cries of distress. He had heard of sales of slaves at auction, but had never seen one, therefore he went in to see for himself. The result of what he saw there changed his mind in that matter; no amount of ignorance and social degradation could balance the horrors of the slave auction, especially as the few advantages that some of them had enjoyed for improvement and culture only tended to increase the wretchedness of the poor slaves. He was a man of ardent piety and tender feelings. His love to God wrought in him a love for all His people created in His image, and for whom He made the sacrifice of His Son for their salvation, therefore, by the time he reached the hospitable mansion of the planter, he had prepared in his mind a sermon suited to the subject that he had seen illustrated at the slave auction.

On his arrival great joy was expressed by all the family; negro boys were mounted on horses and sent in all directions to give notice of a meeting to be held in the evening at the log meeting house in the woods, on the edge of the plantation. Mrs. P and her daughters, happy in having the privilege of doing something for the missionary who had sacrificed so much in so good a cause, commenced making the aforesaid shirts, of which he was in sore need. When the hour for services to commence arrived, the house was filled with the planters and their families from all the country around. The missionary had not mentioned his morning's adventure—he felt troubled, and had a ship been there going to "Tarshish" he might possibly have been tempted to take a voyage in that direction, as did the prophet of old, but he was not the man to shirk responsibility. His text was Isaiah, Chapter 58, 6th verse: "Is not this the fast that I have chosen, to loose the bonds of wickedness, to undo the heavy burdens, to let the oppressed go free, and that ye break every yoke?" There were no shorthand reporters there, and no copy of the sermon is preserved, but he was not the man to "daub with untempered mortar," and the reader is left to judge what kind of a discourse such a man would preach from such a text, having just witnessed a slave auction, and its effect on a slaveholding audience. Twenty years later the preacher would have been lynched, but at that time the ideas that prevailed in 1776 were still held, even in the slave States—that slavery would be abolished gradually by all the States, therefore some of the slaveholders were pleased with the chastisement they had received, thinking it might do good, among whom was brother P—— himself; but his wife and daughters saw it in another light. They were terribly indignant; they would put up with no such meddling with their affairs, and gave notice that not another stitch would they take on those shirts. All this Mr. R—— heard as they walked home through the woods, so on their arrival at the house, at 10 o'clock p. m., he asked for his horse. Mr. P—— remonstrated against his leaving that night, but the ladies grew more and more bitter in their denunciations, and Mr. P—— finally ordered the horse, bidding our friend farewell with many apologies and regrets, and he started, leaving behind his unfinished shirts. Having finished his tour, he arrived home some three months after, but said nothing about the above incident except to his wife, until some six months afterward, when he received from Mr. P——a letter to the following purport:

PLANTATION NEAR CHARLESTON, S. C.,
JANUARY, 18—.

Dear Brother R——: It is impossible for me to express my shame and regret at the inhospitable treatment you received at my house in July last, but much as I have suffered in view of those shameful transactions, it is more than compensated for by the glorious results. You cannot have forgotten the thrilling account you gave us of the agony of that slave mother whose infant child was torn from her arms and dashed upon the ground because the speculator who bought her would not buy the child, nor be burdened with it even as a gift. That scene seemed to be obliterated from the minds of the ladies present by your subsequent denunciations of the institution by which women are relieved of their burdens, though it also entails upon them untold sorrows, hence the rude treatment you received, for which my wife and daughters most humbly ask your forgiveness. When you had been gone a few days, Mrs. P——began to be haunted night and day by a recollection of your description of that scene, but said nothing about it until she awoke one night, screaming and greatly agitated. Seeming disinclined to tell what had frightened her, she again fell asleep, and again awoke still more agitated. She wept so as to be unable to talk for a long time, but when she could speak, she said; "Is it possible that such scenes ever transpire as were described by Elder R?" "Yes," I said, "they are common. Why? what made you think of that now?" She replied: "I have dreamed twice to-night that I witnessed the sale at auction of our Mary. They made her stand on a table, and all the men present were allowed to handle her in the most shameful and immodest manner, which seemed to give her the most excruciating torture, but she bore it without a word until they tore her baby from her and dashed it into a corner of the room, when she fell from the table in convulsions, while the men laughed and urged on the sale of others. Oh, my God, forgive me! I shall never dare to go to sleep again while we own a slave,"—and she never did.

The next morning I went to Charleston and manumitted all our people. They are now our hired servants. We have learned already that free paid labor is cheaper than slave labor, besides the happiness which comes of doing right. I have not before conceived it possible to enjoy, in this life, the happiness that this act of justice has brought into our house. I believe if all our people could be made to realize the joy of doing right, by undoing a most terrible wrong, they would do as I have done. The sense of safety and peace, no patrol in our streets, no weapons under our pillows, no fear of insurrection, no fearful looking for judgment. Oh! my dear sir! if I could but hope to see the day when, in all our country, all men shall live together as brothers, when we shall have equal rights before the law, so that the poor and ignorant shall have protection against oppression from the more intelligent and wealthy classes, my faith in the stability of our institutions, and the ability of our government to sustain itself, would be unbounded. Remembering with Christian affection your faithfulness and moral courage, I remain, Yours, &c.

When alluding to these incidents, the old gentleman used to say, "since then I have never smoothed off the corners of truth to save my shirts." These incidents, related in his pathetic language, made a deep impression on my mind in childhood, but much would have escaped my memory had I not heard them repeated by his widow just before she died, some years ago, in Fredonia, where some of his family still reside. Some of the children who sat around the old gentleman, and listened to his relation of the above and other equally interesting stories, have since been among the most active agents of the U. G. R. R. Some of them were engaged in the "Jerry rescue," one of them is now stumping the State of Illinois for Grant & Colfax, and for their zeal in the cause of God and humanity, loyalty and liberty, much is due to the impressions fixed in their minds while sitting, at the feet of that good man.

CHAPTER XX. REV. J. W. LOGUEN—HIS TRIAL AND RELEASE— LECTURES IN CHAUTAUQUA COUNTY—UNEXPECTED CORROBORATION.

The great central depot of the institution in this State was in Onondaga County, where a great many fugitives were protected, fed and clothed, and sent on their way rejoicing by that noble man, Rev. J. W. Loguen. Mr. Loguen was himself a fugitive. I am not able to relate the particular incidents of his escape, though I have heard him lecture several times, as he said little about himself or his personal adventures. He is respected and beloved by all classes in Syracuse, where he has lived many years, and no other man could have done so much for the U. G. R. R. as he did, yet his friends did not deem it safe for him to remain there after the enactment of the fugitive slave law, but he could not be induced to leave. He was arrested for setting that law at defiance, and aiding in the rescue of the slave Jerry, and was tried for the offense in Albany. The jury disagreed, and he was tried again in Canandaigua, with the same result. The man who claimed him as a slave knew where he was, and Mr. Loguen's friends feared that he would be seized by government officials when beyond the protection of the friends who surrounded him at his home, but he always said that "he apprehended no danger; if the old man wanted him he hoped he would come himself, but if he thought it best to send somebody else, it was all the same to him. He was not going to Canada or to Tennessee, nor would he ask the aid of his friends, but he gave notice to all concerned that he should trust in *Loguen* and in Providence for protection, and principally and first of all in Loguen."

When the Presidential campaign of 1852 was in progress, Mr. Loguen was invited to speak in a certain village in Chautauqua Co., on the lake shore. He had a large audience, and delivered an eloquent address.

Some person asked him to relate his adventures in making his escape from slavery. He respectfully declined saying anything about himself, but spoke of the sufferings endured by his sister, which he witnessed, but could do nothing to protect her. Because she would not submit to his brutal conduct, her master tied her thumbs together, and with a cord over a pulley, drew her up until she stood on her toes, then whipped her bare back until she fainted. As soon as she could go she ran away. The old fellow overtook her ten miles from home, tied a rope around her neck and made her run home. When she became exhausted and fell, he would drag her by the neck, then wait until she could stand up and start again. This was a pretty hard story, and it was not strange that the audience did not all believe it. When Mr. Loguen sat down, a man arose and said he did not believe the story, and denounced the speaker for uttering the slander. After he sat down, a gentleman near the door arose and said he should like to say a few words. He began by saying that he lived in Stewart Co., Tennessee, near Cumberland, where the speaker said he came from, and where his sister was so shockingly abused. He should have said nothing but for the remarks of the last speaker, who doubted the statement of Mr. Loguen, "but," said he, "having lived in Tennessee all my life, I regret to have to say that *I do not doubt the story*. He told it as no man could have told it who had not seen it. I would not say that such cruelty is common, but it is too frequent not to be known to any man who has lived among slaves. I thank you, Mr. Chairman, for allowing a stranger to indorse the veracity of the speaker." Of course, Mr. Loguen's character was vindicated, for the man was a slaveholder, and even a Democrat could not object to his testimony.

At the close of the meeting the last named gentleman sought an interview with Mr. Loguen, and told him that he was stopping in town over night, and learning that a colored man was going to speak, he had come to hear what he had to say, "and," he said, "I could do no less than

I did, as the people here seem to know nothing of our ways." After talking awhile about men and things in Tennessee, he asked Mr. Loguen the name of the man he had lived with in Cumberland. Mr. Loguen declined answering the question, when the gentleman said, "You need have no fear of me, I shall not hurt you." "I presume not," said Loguen, "but since the fugitive slave law was passed my friends advise me to go to Canada, or to some place where I am not known as a fugitive, but I am going to stay where I choose to stay, and go where I choose to go, and I hope no one will ever try to enforce that law on me, not that I fear anything for myself, but *somebody will get hurt"*

Large rewards in cash and political honors awaited the delivery of Loguen in Tennessee, and there were Democrats enough who wanted them, but nobody ever got the rewards, for both Loguen and Providence stood in the way. Loguen was a prophet, a type of our times, and has lived to seethe prophecy fulfilled. "The lost cause" offered all the offices and all the treasure of the nation for the delivery of all the people, both white and black, into the hands of the slave power, but Grant & Colfax stood in the way; the nation is safe; nobody will be hurt.

The remote influences that have worked in the hearts of the people, leading on to their final results in establishing the U. G. R. R., as related briefly in this sketch, were suggested to my memory by the open declaration by the party of Seymour and Blair in the South, that their election would restore to them all that they fought for in the rebellion, and inaugurate all the barbarities of slavery. Can Christians, then, vote for such men? Can they speak, act, and vote in favor of annulling the word of God and our Declaration of Independence? Not unless their souls are so encased in copper that no ray of light has illuminated them in these many years. The election of Grant is liberty and peace.

CHAPTER XXI. THE SOUTHERN U. G. R. R.—IT'S USE DURING THE WAR—A UNION PRISONER'S EXPERIENCE ESCAPING FROM ANDERSONVILLE.

It has been hinted that the lines of this road were extended from time to time, until they reached far into the slave States, and that the experience and information of the conductors enabled them to render aid to our soldiers when escaping from rebel prisons, that could not have been had from any other source. W. E— was one of a large lot of prisoners who were put into that horrible pen at Andersonville. He enlisted in a regiment that went from northern Illinois under General Hurlbut, though he was born, and lived until he was sixteen years old, in Perrysburgh, Cattaraugus Co. I knew him well—the last time I saw him was at Belvidere, Ill., soon after his return. When he entered the prison at twenty years of age, few men could boast of a more hardy constitution, but he was starved to a mere skeleton, reduced from 172 pounds weight to less than 70 pounds. He reached home, but never recovered. He died soon after, and said he should have died in prison had he not *"determined he would not;"* his indomitable "pluck "kept him alive. The brutalities inflicted on the prisoners, and the systematic starvation to which they were subjected by the Southern Democrats who came up to New York to aid Northern Copperheads in making a platform and nominating candidates for President and Vice-President, defy description. The scanty rations, less than one sixth the amount required to sustain men in healthy condition, often consisted of raw corn, or what is still worse, corn and cobs ground together, and no fuel was allowed to cook it. Then they would place small sticks of wood just over the dead line; one day one of E——'s comrades reached across the fatal line to get a stick to use in cooking his cob meal; the crack of a gun was heard, and the body of the poor fellow lay stretched across the line, from whence his comrades could not remove him without subjecting themselves to the same penalty. The camp was surrounded with timber, but they were never allowed a quarter of a supply for cooking, still less to keep them warm in winter. They were without tents or shelter of any kind. Had they been allowed the privilege they would have brought timber from the woods and made shanties for themselves, but this was denied them. Several men were shot in trying to reach across the dead line to get a little *clean* water, none fit to use being within reach elsewhere.

Great numbers of these unfortunate prisoners had been stripped of their boots and all their clothing, and received in return a ragged shirt and pants, without blanket or overcoat, with no shelter whatever. They dug holes in the ground to keep warm in, from whence they were often driven out by water on stormy nights, and as the result, thirty dead bodies were often gathered up in the morning. No class of human beings have been found in any country, claiming to be civilized, who have been guilty of such horrid atrocities, except in communities where slavery existed, and strange as it may seem, it is always the oppressor and not the oppressed who suffers this moral degradation, as will be seen in the relation of a few incidents.

Our friend W. E—— never succeeded in escaping from prison; he was released at the close of the war, but some escaped, and after several weeks were re-captured and returned to prison. One of them in relating his adventures, said: "We crossed the Saluda River and lay in the woods until dark; then in trying to find the road to Greenville, passing a gate we heard some one call out, 'Who's dar?' Presuming it was a negro, we stopped, and one of the party went to see who it was and inquire the way. It was an old negro woman. When she saw us she said, 'You's Yanks, 'scaped from prison. I seen 'em 'fore, and feed 'em, but now I'm gwine to de riber and can't go back.' She directed them on the road to Greenville, and said, 'Go careful, make no noise. About three miles farther on we met an old negro who had started to go some ten miles to spend the Sabbath with his wife. I asked him if he had ever heard of the Yankees. 'Yes,' said he, 'we hear bout dem people. Massa G—— tell us bery bad tings bout dem, but can't tell bout dat ar after all.' 'Did you ever see any of them?' 'No, widout you is some.' 'If I should tell you that we are Yankees, would you believe it, and would you give us something to eat?' 'Ob course I would believe you; go with me.' He went back with us three miles, and after secreting us in the bushes he went away saying, 'I return in an hour, then I cough to let you know it's me. If anybody come and don't cough, keep bery still, dat ain't *me*.' In about an hour we heard some one coughing as if he were in the last stages of consumption. Presently the old man appeared, loaded with bread, bacon, sweet potatoes, and some salt. He then went two miles with us. Before he left us I asked him if he knew what the Yankees were doing for them. 'Oh, yes,' said he, 'we knows all 'bout dat. You's our frens. Massa Linkum make us all free by proclamation.'

" 'Who is this 'Massa Linkum' of whom you speak?' " 'He is d'e President who's been 'lected by de people, but the rebs refuse de knowledge ob it, and make Jeff Davis President.'

" 'Don't you think Jeff Davis is abetter President than Lincoln?'

"Shaking his head and exposing his ivory, he said, 'Better nor Linkum, what's been' lected by the people, what's 'titled to the posishun, what's made us all free? Can't tell dese chil'n anyting'bout dat. Dey knows all' bout it.'

"This man's name was Frank. He had been willing to forego his visit to his wife, procured a large supply of food, went five miles with us on our way, and felt that he was more than paid in having had the privilege of doing a favor to 'Massa Linkum's sogers.'"

After leaving the old man, keeping in the road, they went toward Greenville until two o'clock in the morning, when they came suddenly on a negro in the road with a large bundle under his arm. He refused to tell what he had in his bundle, but on learning that they were Yankees, he said, 'I've had no meat in forty days. I got dese chickens for my Sunday dinner, but de Yankees are friends to us and we friends to dem. Now dem's my words, take 'em." Three or four days after this, becoming very hungry, they were on the lookout for negroes, knowing that there was no safety in applying to any others. Having made a camp at daylight, one of them crept carefully toward a field, and soon saw five negroes come into the field and commence plowing. In going around they passed near him, and when he saw that there was no white man with them, he rapped on the fence, whereupon they all stopped, and one of the negroes said, "Gor a mighty! How comes you dar? Who is ye? whar ye come from?" Cautioning them to make no noise, the narrator said, "I want to talk with one of you, and the rest keep about your work." The negroes appointed a man to talk with him, and the rest went on with their work. Questioning the negro, he learned that his name was Phil; that Phil's master was an officer, on duty in Charlestown, "banking up against the Yankees," as Phil expressed it, where some of them had been killed and others wounded by the Yankee shells. "Well now, Phil," said our friend, "did you ever see a Yankee?"

"No, sah."

"I suppose you think they are bad people?"

"No, sah. De Yankees is de friends ob de black people."

"How do you know that the, Yankees are your friends?"

"Oh, we hear massa talking 'bout it. He call 'em d d abolitionists. We knows what dat means."

"What do you understand by an abolitionist?"

"Means de—de year ob jubilee am comin', when we's all gwine to be free."

"Well, Phil, that is a very good definition; but who told you that you are to be made free?"

"Oh, we gets it."

"Well, Ph'il, I am a Yankee; can you do anything for me?"

"I knowed ye was. Do any ting? what ye want done? I can do ebery ting?"

"I want something to eat, and there are more of us. How many can you feed."

"I can feed an army of ye," said Phil. Phil was getting excited.

With extreme caution they crept through the bushes to where they had camped for the day. Some conversation was had in which Phil asked anxiously if the slaves were really going to be made free, and being assured that Lincoln's proclamation had made them all free, and that a million of them had their liberty already, he said, "Massa says yon are gwine to sell us all to Cuba, but we don't believe it." "No, Phil, not one of you will be sold. We are going to make men of you; send your children to school, and teach you to read. Now, Phil, is this a safe place for us to stay?" "Yes," said Phil, "if you keeps bery still. I comes to-night and brings you to a better place, and gibs you all de provisions you want." He bounded away, and well nigh forgot himself in singing,

> "De kingdom am a comin'
> And de year ob jubilee."

One of the party called to him and said, "*Still*, my boy, *still*." "Oh, yes sah, I forgot," and he was soon out of sight. Phil was as good as his word. He came to them as soon as it was dark, conducted them to an old house, brought them more food than they could eat and carry away, and also brought a negro shoemaker, who mended their shoes, and several old negroes to talk with them. When they started on late in the evening, Phil went with them. When out of hearing of those left in the house, Phil startled them with the question, "Massa, does you tink you can find the way to Tennessee? Mighty long way dar, and bery crooked road, and now, I tinks you had better take a guide wid you, to show you de way. I knows de way from heah to Knoxville." "No," they said, "we are prisoners of war, and liable to be caught any hour, and should we be caught and you be found with us, they would hang us all. Direct us the best route to go and we will take the risk. Your time will come soon, Phil, you will be free. God bless you." Phil seemed to have a foreboding of trouble, and would willingly have risked his own life to help them on to Knoxville. Had he been allowed to go they might have avoided the ambush into which they fell the next day.

They were sent back to prison, not, however, to Andersonville, for Sherman was already on his march to the sea, but they were sent to Columbia, and afterwards with other prisoners transferred from place to place until the final surrender at Appomattox.

The first years of the war the lines were kept open along the Shenandoah, through Maryland, through West Virginia, along the mountains in Tennessee, and wherever Union prisoners needed guides, but later in the war the raids of Stoneman, Sheridan and others had picked up and appropriated the most intelligent guides. Yet the time never came during the war when prisoners trying to escape were not safe for the time being in trusting themselves to the guidance of negroes.

CHAPTER XXII.FRIGHTENED MOSES—EXPECTING TO BE KILLED AND EATEN BY ABOLITIONISTS.

One thing was always observable, by which we knew a fugitive slave from an imposter, namely, a restless, sharp sense of danger, a sudden start if a person was heard approaching the house, while the opening of a door or the barking of a dog would produce in them intense excitement.

One of our most active agents lived in the town of New Haven, Oswego Co., within sight of Lake Ontario. He was a farmer by the name of French. Going, one evening, to return his cows to the pasture, he saw a man in the woods suddenly coming into sight, and then trying to hide. Going towards him, the man moved off, but seemed unable to run from some cause. French ran towards him and told him to stop. As he approached he saw that the man was a negro, and thinking he was a fugitive, said to him, "Don't be afraid, I am an abolitionist;" whereupon the poor fellow put forth all the strength he had to effect his escape, but it was a feeble effort, and he soon fell to the ground. When Mr. French came up to him the man began begging for his life. "Don't be frightened," said French, "we are all abolitionists in this neighborhood." "Yes, massa," said the negro, "but den ye see I'se good for nuffin, I'se so pore, only bones and skin; I'se eat nuffin amost dese six weeks—do massa, let me lib!" "Come with me," said Mr. French, "and I will feed you and take care of you," He tried to beg off, but was too weak to resist, and French took him home. Mrs. French prepared for him an excellent supper, but he could not be induced to taste of it. The sight of food seemed to distress him; he was evidently starving, but was afraid to eat. It was a singular case; French could not understand it. He repeatedly told him that they were all abolitionists, which frightened the negro almost out of his senses. Finally, Mrs. French made the remark that the slaves were sometimes told that the abolitionists are cannibals. "Talk with him," said she, "and find out what he is afraid of." Mr. French talked kindly to him, telling how many fugitives he had assisted and sent them to Canada. "Dey so pore," pleaded the negro, "dey good for nuffin! I'se pore, too—do, massa, let me go!" "Yes," said French, "I will send you to Canada, but you must stay here till you are able to go. You are starved; eat something and go to sleep; we will talk more about it in the morning." "No," he replied, "I rather die than be killed and eat up." French saw that some terrible fear was controlling the poor fellow, and determined to ascertain what it was. It required a long continued and patient effort to induce the negro to tell the cause of his fear. When he had done so his friends soon found means to dispel his fears, and he ate all that was deemed safe for him, and was put on a comfortable bed, from which he did not get up for many weeks. He was so far gone when French found him that one or two more days of starvation would have finished him. Had he not been taken in when he was, he must have died in the woods.

In Georgia, where Moses (he said they called him Mose) lived, the slaves were partially educated. Their mothers taught them a short lesson in astronomy, namely, the position of the north star and how to find it. Their masters lectured them on the manners and customs of dogs and men; when one of them ran off he was hunted with dogs; when baffled in the pursuit and the slave escaped, the fact was never acknowledged, but the slaves were called together and told how the fugitive had been torn in pieces by the dogs and left to rot in the woods, and the occasion was generally improved by telling them how much better it was for the poor negro to be killed by the dogs than it would have been to fall into the hands of the savage abolitionists, a kind of people living in the North, who, when they could catch a negro, would fatten him, if he would eat, and then kill and eat him. Such was their education. It will be readily understood, that there were two reasons why Moses, when found by our enterprising agent, was so nearly famished. First, his journey had been prolonged many weeks by his fear of falling into the hands of the abolitionists, so that he had gone all the way to the shore of Lake Ontario without having been seen by any of our agents; and second, he thought that if he was very "pore" the cannibal abolitionists would regard him as of no account, and let him go. It may be doubted that any slave was ever so ignorant as to believe such stories, but many of them have spoken of having been told the same thing, and it is not strange that some of them believed it. Moses had but a short ride on our cars, and shipped for Kingston, C. W., on a lumber vessel, from the mouth of Salmon River.

CHAPTER XXIII.ONEDA LACKOW'S FLIGHT FROM ALABAMA— CAPTURE AND ESCAPE—THE FAITHFUL DOG—THE KIND- HEARTED JAILER'S WIFE—GRADUATES FROM A SEMINARY AND GOES TO ENGLAND.

Oneda Lackow was a servant in the house of her master on a plantation in Alabama, on the bank of the Mobile River. She seems to have been a favorite in the family, a sprightly, intelligent girl. Her features, hair and complexion would not have betrayed her as a slave except in a country where such slaves are common. Being a young lady's maid she had many opportunities for improvement, and suffered few of the privations incident to the life of a slave. Instead of making her satisfied with her condition, the privileges she enjoyed served to make her feel more keenly the degradation of slavery, and she resolved, when not more than ten years of age, to escape to a land of freedom or die in the attempt. While she kept her purpose a secret, she availed herself of every opportunity to obtain information that would be useful when she should start for some free country. Her young mistress had been educated in New England, and she often heard her talk about the free States. Oneda learned to read, and was shrewd enough to conceal the fact from her mistress, therefore she had frequent opportunities to read papers and study a map of the United States that hung in the hall. When she was twelve or thirteen years old, her master brought home a young dog of the St. Bernard breed. His name was Prince, and he was trained to watch the premises. The first time she saw the great, clumsy looking puppy, she said to herself, (she told her plans to no one but herself,) "Now I'll pet this dog and make him love me, and some day we will escape together;" so whenever opportunity favored she encouraged the children, both white and black, to tease Prince and abuse him, when she would come to the rescue, drive away the children, and then pet and feed him. She contrived to feed him such things as he liked best, and to play with him every day, and at night she would sometimes lie down by him on the piazza, lay her head on him and go to sleep, so that when Prince was two years old he would come or go at her bidding, though she was careful never to exercise her control of him in the presence of her master. When she was about fifteen years old she had laid down one evening on the porch with Prince, and happened to overhear a conversation between her master and a trader, and to her astonishment she learned that her market value was more than any two of the strongest men on the plantation, and that in a year or two more her master expected to obtain a much larger price for her. She had never been treated harshly, yet the degradation of her condition was seldom absent from her thoughts. Not many days after the incident above related, her master and mistress went to Mobile to be absent a week. The next night, when all was still about the house, Oneda, with a little package containing a few articles of clothing and some food, went silently out of the house, and passing near to where Prince was lying, he followed her. She took a road leading west towards the Mobile & Ohio R. R., then striking a road running directly north, she turned into it and went on all night. Prince became excited, and tried in his mute way to induce her to turn back, though he seemed to be determined to go with her wherever she might go.

It would be interesting to follow this heroic girl through her long, lonely journey through Alabama, Tennessee, and Kentucky to the Ohio River, sometimes camping in woods and swamps in the daytime, and traveling by the north star in the night, occasionally finding, a resting place in a negro's cabin, hungry, weary and footsore. With no companion but her faithful dog, with no thought of turning back or of stopping short of freedom, she went on for three long months. She was often in great danger of being arrested and sent back, but, sometimes by the aid of her faithful escort, Prince, sometimes aided by negroes, and once or twice by kindhearted white women, she eluded her pursuers and arrived safely in Ohio, having been once captured and escaped again in Kentucky. Some of her adventures are worthy of notice, one or two of which I will relate.

She was near the mountain passes in Kentucky, having been traveling nearly eleven weeks, and was already near the Southern terminus of the U. G. R. R., when, driven by hunger, she went into a house in a lonely place, hoping to find it occupied by negroes, but was disappointed in finding a white woman. She noticed a singular expression in the woman's countenance when Prince followed her into the house, but was too hungry and tired to think much of it. She asked for food, and the woman gave her something to eat, which she divided with Prince. The woman noticed her shoes, and said to her, "Your shoes are worn out," and stepping into another room she said, "come in here and see if these will fit you. If you can wear them I'll give them to you." She went in, and as Prince was following her, the woman shut the door against him, locked the door, and put the key in her pocket; then taking a clothes line that hung in the room, she said, "you must stay here until my man comes home, and to make a sure thing of it, I must tie your feet and hands." She was a great, coarse creature, and the child knew that resistance would avail nothing, while her voice and manner gave no encouragement to appeal for pity, but she thought of Prince and began calling him, screaming as loud as she could. Prince howled and scratched at the door, to which the woman paid no attention, but took hold of her and began arranging the cords. Oneda resisted with what strength she had, and they both fell upon the floor, when, with an awful yell, Prince came crashing through a window, breaking glass and sash, and seized the woman by the throat. The contest had been unequal before Prince took part in it, and it was no less so now. Prince had the advantage, and would have made an end of it at once, but Oneda said, "Easy, Prince, hold on there;" she then said to the woman, "Don't resist,

if you do he will kill you." She had her enemy somewhat as Grant had Buckner at Donelson, terms "unconditional surrender." "Now," said she to the woman, "you must submit to me. If you are quiet while I use these cords it will be well for you, but if you stir up strife here Prince will interfere, and if he gets hold of you again I may not be able to restrain him. You must lie still while I say to you a few words, and first of all, let me tell you that the grip of Prince's jaws on your neck is a pleasant pastime for you, compared with the suffering you propose to inflict on me; and the bondage that you must submit to will be but for a day, whereas you would bind me in slavery for life." She then tied her hands behind her back and her feet together, and filled her mouth with an apron to prevent her from calling for help. "Now," said she, "you are in bondage; I won't ask you how you like it, but I reckon' you will be an abolitionist by the time your 'man' comes home." She found on a shelf some crusts of bread and scraps of cold meat, which she wrapped in a newspaper that she found in the room, and started off. She had become weak from hunger and exposure, but her fears seemed to give her new strength. The road was lonely, passing ravines in the hills and woods; when she saw anybody in the road she hid herself until they had passed by and then ran forward, until late in the day, when she turned away from the road and sat down to rest. On opening her package of food to feed Prince, she saw at the head of an advertisement a wood cut, the figure of a slave escaping, and read as follows:
$450 REWARD.
Ran away from my plantation on the Mobile River, thirty miles from the city of Mobile, my slave girl, Oneda. She left on the 3d of June, 185—, and took with her a very large black dog. The girl is fifteen years of age, has long hair, brown eyes, and brunette complexion, rather less than medium size, but remarkably well formed, smiles when she speaks and shows a dimple in her left cheek, is very intelligent, and is supposed to be able to read. Any person who will capture and secure

them in any jail south of the Ohio River, so that I can get them, will receive $300 reward, and if *carefully handled so that the dog be not maimed nor the person of the girl disfigured*, $150 will be added to the above reward.

James L——.

The paper was directed to J. Tice, Piketon, Pike Co., Ky. "This explains it all," said Oneda. "That will do, my brother, your powers of description are truly remarkable—*'is supposed to be able to read'*—of course she can read, and then, too, you appeal to the sordid instincts of a brutal slave catcher, to save me from physical suffering, while you, regardless of fraternal relationship, would degrade my humanity, and hold in base chattel slavery your own sister. I'll take care of this," said she, as she put the paper in her pocket. "Prince, my good fellow, come here—lie down by me and keep me warm. You are not my brother, Prince, you are only a dog. I've read somewhere that in Turkey they call Christians dogs; I wonder if dogs are ever Christians. Oh, Prince! what is the difference betwixt you and me?" Her soliloquy was cut short by Prince; he sprang up and took an attitude of defense, looked around at her with a low whine, and then was about to spring forward. She spoke to him and he came close to her side and licked her face; she looked up and saw a man not more than forty feet off, holding a blood-hound by a rope and a rifle on his shoulder. She sprang to her feet, and putting her hand on Prince's head, she exclaimed, "Stand off, or Prince shall kill both you and your dog!" Making instant preparations to use his gun, he said, "We'll talk this matter over. You see I have a right smart chance of advantage. Here are two of us and two dogs, and then you see, here is this gun. I have come after you, and I reckon you are a sensible girl, and will go along with me without compelling me to shoot that dog." Oneda saw the point at once, and proposed to surrender, though not without conditions. After a long parley it was agreed that she should be taken to the Piketon jail, and that Prince should remain with her. He then untied his hound and sent him home. It was now almost dark, and as they went toward the town, which was not far off, she said, "This is Mr. Tice, I suppose." "Yes," said he, "Jake Tice, known from the Ohio River to the gulf as the great slave catcher. Ye see, this is the run-way, and if a slave runs off they just send the papers to me. If ye'd knowed that I reckon ye'd 'a gone the other side of the mountain." "Have you just come from home?" asked Oneda. "Yes," said Tice, "I jest ondid the old woman, and let loose her jaw, and wasn't she mad, do you think? Wal, she wasn't—that is, not much. She was mighty sorry for ye, but then ye see, there was the $300, and more, too, on conditions, ye know, and business has been mighty dull all summer. She said you had but just started, and I could follow your track with the old hound, 'but you must tie him,' said the old woman, 'or somebody will get killed sure.' " "I was sorry," said Oneda, "to have to do as I did, but I could not help it." It was with great difficulty that she walked to the town, and when they got there, Randall, the jailer, asked Tice to stay till morning, and then they would write to Mr. L—— to come after his slave. Tice was an easy going fellow, and boasted that he never did a cruel thing when he could avoid it. Randall's family lived in the jail, and Tice said to Mrs. Randall, "This poor child is tired out and starved. You give her a good supper and let her sleep on a bed; we won't lock her in a cell to-night." Mrs. Randall objected at first, saying she would not be responsible for her safe keeping. Tice, laughing, said "her Prince would see to that." In the morning Tice and the jailer went into the office and wrote a letter, notifying her master that Oneda and Prince were both safe in Pike County jail, but before mailing the letter they went to her room and she was gone. Mrs. Randall could give no account of her; she had put her in bed as directed, and that was all she could say about it; if she had got away she was glad of it, for, said she, "that girl has no more *right* to be a slave than I have. She is whiter than any of us." A blood-hound was procured and taken to her room, and after smelling around, he took her track, being led by a cord, and went directly to the west fork of the Big Sandy, which runs through the town. Beyond that the hound could find no track, and it was decided that she must have taken a light skiff that usually laid at the crossing and gone down the river, and two hours after the boat was found capsized among some rocks below the rapids. So the letter to Mr. L——was burned up and Tice went home.

In the back yard of the jail there was a pit where a well had been commenced a long time ago, and abandoned for some cause when about eight feet deep. It was covered over with boards, and a short ladder had been left standing in it. After all was still about the premises, Mrs. Randall carried blankets and old clothes into it, and then went into Oneda's room. After awhile they went out, walked to the river, sent the skiff adrift and returned, went through the house, and Oneda and Prince went into the pit, after which Mrs. Randall carefully replaced the boards. She kept them well supplied with food for ten days, and then sent them towards Ohio by an old negro who lived alone just out of town, and was often absent for a week or two without being missed. Thenceforth she was hungry no more, nor did she travel without a guide. The U. G. R. R. took her direct to Canada by way of Cleveland, and by steamboat to Malden. After spending a few months in the Wilberforce Colony, Oneda returned to Ohio for the purpose of attending school. Prince was left in Canada, having become domesticated in a kind family. Oneda graduated at a popular seminary in Ohio, and then went to England, taking with her letters of introduction from the professors of the seminary. When on her way to New York, where she was to embark, she spent a week at our house.

In these brief sketches, no attempt has been made to give more than an outline of a few incidents connected with each case, and of many thousands who escaped from slavery by the aid of the U. G. R. R., only some twenty or thirty have been alluded to. Of what they suffered before they started, little has been written.

Their heroic achievements in effecting their escape against the terrible odds arrayed against them, and their enterprise and success in establishing for themselves homes, schools and churches, challenges the admiration of all good men.

Made in the USA
Monee, IL
13 March 2021